Ms McCulloch

BOOK 4

Prim-Ed
Publishing
www.prim-ed.com

Grammar minutes

100 minutes to practise and reinforce essential skills

Carmen S Jones

6330

Grammar minutes *Book 4*

Published by Prim-Ed Publishing® 2011 under licence to
Creative Teaching Press.
Copyright© 2009 Creative Teaching Press.
This version copyright© Prim-Ed Publishing® 2011

ISBN 978-1-84654-297-8
PR–6330

Titles available in this series:

Grammar minutes Book 1
Grammar minutes Book 2
Grammar minutes Book 3
Grammar minutes Book 4
Grammar minutes Book 5
Grammar minutes Book 6

Internet websites

In some cases, websites or specific URLs may be recommended. While these are checked and rechecked at the time of publication, the publisher has no control over any subsequent changes which may be made to webpages. It is *strongly* recommended that the class teacher checks *all* URLs before allowing pupils to access them.

View all pages online

Website: www.prim-ed.com

GRAMMAR MINUTES – BOOK 4

Foreword

Grammar minutes is a six-book series for primary school pupils that provides a structured daily programme of easy-to-follow activities in grammar. The main objective is grammar proficiency, attained by teaching pupils to apply grammar skills to answer questions effortlessly and rapidly. The questions in this book provide pupils with practice in the following key areas of grammar instruction:

- *sentence structure*
- *nouns*
- *pronouns*
- *adverbs*
- *prefixes/suffixes*
- *prepositions*
- *capital letters*
- *verbs*
- *adjectives*
- *subjects/predicates*
- *abbreviations/punctuation.*

Grammar minutes – Book 4 features 100 'minutes', each with 10 classroom-tested problems. Use this comprehensive resource to improve your pupils' overall grammar proficiency, which will promote greater self-confidence in their grammar skills as well as provide the everyday practice necessary to succeed in testing situations. Designed to be implemented in numerical order from 1 to 100, the activities in *Grammar minutes* are developmental through each book and across the series.

Comprehensive teachers notes, record-keeping charts, a scope-and-sequence table (showing when each new concept and skill is introduced) and photocopiable pupil reference materials are also included.

How many minutes does it take to complete a 'grammar minute'?

Pupils will enjoy challenging themselves as they apply their grammar knowledge and understanding to complete a 'grammar minute' in the fastest possible time.

Titles available in this series:

- *Grammar minutes – Book 1*
- *Grammar minutes – Book 2*
- *Grammar minutes – Book 3*
- *Grammar minutes – Book 4*
- *Grammar minutes – Book 5*
- *Grammar minutes – Book 6*

Contents

Teachers notes

How to use this book

Grammar minutes can be used in a variety of ways, such as:

- **a speed test**. As the teacher starts a stopwatch, pupils begin the 'minute'. As each pupil finishes, he/she raises a hand and the teacher calls out the time. The pupil records this time on the appropriate place on the sheet. Alternatively, a particular time can be allocated for the whole class to complete the 'minute' in.
  Pupils record their scores and time on their 'minute journal' (see page vii).
- **a whole-class activity**. Work through the 'minute' together as a teaching or reviewing activity.
- **a warm-up activity**. Use a 'minute' a day as a 'starter' or warm-up activity before the main part of the lesson begins.
- **a homework activity**. If given as a homework activity, it would be most beneficial for the pupils if the 'minute' is corrected and reviewed at the start of the following lesson.

Grammar minutes strategies

Encourage pupils to apply the following strategies to help improve their scores and decrease the time taken to complete the 10 questions.

- To use strategies whenever possible.
- To move quickly down the page, answering the problems they know first.
- To come back to problems they are unsure of, after they have completed all other problems.
- To make educated guesses when they encounter problems they are not familiar with.

A *Grammar minute* pupil activity page.

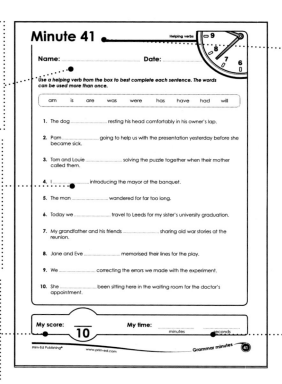

Name and date
Pupils write their name and the date in the spaces provided.

Questions
There are 10 problems, providing practice in every key area of grammar proficiency.

Score
Pupils record their score out of 10 in the space provided.

'Grammar minute' number
Grammar minutes are designed to be completed in numerical order.

Time
Pupils record the time taken to complete the 'minute' at the bottom of the sheet. (This is optional.)

iv Grammar minutes
www.prim-ed.com
Prim-Ed Publishing®

Teachers notes

Marking

Answers are provided for all activities. How these activities are marked will vary according to the teacher's organisational policy. Methods could include whole-class checking, partner checking, individual pupil checking or collection by the teacher.

Diagnosis of problem areas

Grammar minutes provides the teacher with immediate feedback of whole-class and individual pupil understanding. This information is useful for future programming and planning of further opportunities to practise and review the skills and concepts which need addressing.

Make use of the structured nature of the questions to diagnose problem areas; rather than asking who got 10 out of 10, ask the pupils who got Question 1 correct to raise their hands, Question 2, Question 3 etc. In this way, you will be able to quickly determine which concepts are causing problems for the majority of the pupils. Once the routine of *Grammar minutes* is established, the teacher will have time to work with individuals or small groups to assist them with any areas causing problems.

Meeting the needs of individuals

The structure of *Grammar minutes* allows some latitude in the way the books are used; for example, it may be impractical (as well as demoralising for some) for all pupils to be using the same book. It can also be difficult for teachers to manage the range of abilities found in any one classroom, so while pupils may be working at different levels from different books, the familiar structure makes it easier to cope with individual differences. An outline of the suggested age range levels each book is suited to is given on page iii.

Additional resources:

- **Minute records**
  Teachers can record pupil scores and times on the **Minute records** table located on page vi.

- **Scope and sequence**
  The **Scope-and-sequence table** gives the 'minute' in which each new skill and concept appears for the first time.

- **Minute journal**
  Once a 'minute' is completed, pupils record their score and time on their **Minute journal**, located on page vii.

- **Answers to all questions are found on pages 101 to 105.**

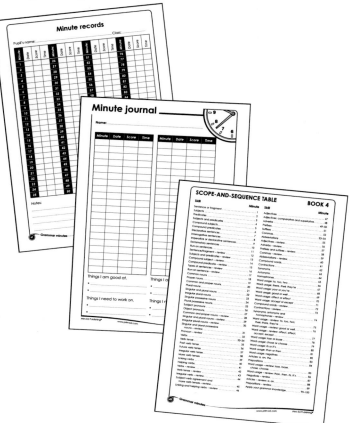

Minute records

Pupil's name: .... Class: ....

Minute:	Date	Score	Time	Minute:	Date	Score	Time	Minute:	Date	Score	Time	Minute:	Date	Score	Time
1				26				51				76			
2				27				52				77			
3				28				53				78			
4				29				54				79			
5				30				55				80			
6				31				56				81			
7				32				57				82			
8				33				58				83			
9				34				59				84			
10				35				60				85			
11				36				61				86			
12				37				62				87			
13				38				63				88			
14				39				64				89			
15				40				65				90			
16				41				66				91			
17				42				67				92			
18				43				68				93			
19				44				69				94			
20				45				70				95			
21				46				71				96			
22				47				72				97			
23				48				73				98			
24				49				74				99			
25				50				75				100			

Notes:

....

....

....

....

Prim-Ed Publishing®

Minute journal

Name: ....

Minute	Date	Score	Time

Minute	Date	Score	Time

Things I am good at.

• ....

• ....

Things I need to work on.

• ....

• ....

Things I am good at.

• ....

• ....

Things I need to work on.

• ....

• ....

SCOPE-AND-SEQUENCE TABLE   BOOK 4

www.prim-ed.com   Prim-Ed Publishing®

Sentence or fragment

Name: .... **Date:** ....

Read each group of words below. If the group of words is a complete sentence, circle sentence. If the group of words is not a complete sentence, circle fragment.

(Hint: Remember that a complete sentence is a group of words that tells a complete thought.)

1. Tony and Danny are going to the Oceanside Aquarium.	**sentence**	**fragment**
2. Are excited about going to see the animals.	**sentence**	**fragment**
3. The boys have saved their pocket money to pay for the tickets.	**sentence**	**fragment**
4. Danny is bringing his new digital camera.	**sentence**	**fragment**
5. Tony is interested in seeing the sea lion.	**sentence**	**fragment**
6. Jumps and does tricks.	**sentence**	**fragment**
7. The boys have fun walking through the Seaside Journey Exhibit.	**sentence**	**fragment**
8. See reef fish and stingrays.	**sentence**	**fragment**
9. Lunch at a deli across the street.	**sentence**	**fragment**
10. The boys can't wait to go back with some more friends.	**sentence**	**fragment**

My score: $\dfrac{}{10}$

My time: ....
minutes   seconds

Minute 2

Name: .... **Date:** ....

Write the subject of each sentence on the line.

*(Hint: The **subject of a sentence** tells who or what the sentence is about. It is usually at the beginning of a sentence.)*

1. We saw flamingos on our class excursion to the zoo.   ....

2. Flamingos are big pink birds with long legs.   ....

3. Some people buy plastic flamingos to put on their lawn.   ....

4. Kyra read that flamingos live in large groups called colonies.   ....

5. The zookeeper showed us a 10 minute DVD about flamingos.   ....

6. Judy was scared of them.   ....

7. Our teacher tried to comfort the crying girls.   ....

8. Female flamingos lay one large white egg per year.   ....

9. Baby flamingos are born with grey and white feathers.   ....

10. Our class really learned a lot about flamingos on our trip.   ....

My score: _____
$\frac{}{10}$

My time: ....
              minutes   seconds

Prim-Ed Publishing®
www.prim-ed.com

Minute 3

Name: .... **Date:** ....

Circle the predicate in each sentence.

*(Hint: The **predicate of a sentence** tells what someone or something is or does. It is usually the last part of a sentence.)*

1. Our school basketball team prepares for our first game.

2. The coach demonstrates how to dribble the ball correctly.

3. Nick blocked the ball from going into the basket.

4. John and Tim were practising their free throws.

5. The coach showed us how to block the offence.

6. I scored a three-pointer right before the buzzer went off.

7. The cheerleaders were also practising in the gym.

8. My sister is the captain of the cheerleading squad.

9. We run laps around the gym to strengthen our legs.

10. The team is ready for the game on Friday.

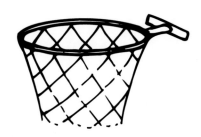

My score: $\dfrac{}{10}$

My time: ....
minutes   seconds

Minute 4

Name: .... Date: ....

Each of these sentences is incomplete. Circle subject *if the subject is missing.* Circle predicate *if the predicate is missing.*

1. The sleeping dog.   **subject**   **predicate**

2. Walks to the refrigerator.   **subject**   **predicate**

3. The woman with the pretty dress.   **subject**   **predicate**

4. Sasha and I.   **subject**   **predicate**

5. Is threading the needle to sew on a button.   **subject**   **predicate**

6. Are under the sink.   **subject**   **predicate**

7. Cried throughout the sad film.   **subject**   **predicate**

8. The boy scouts' uniforms.   **subject**   **predicate**

9. Was slowly fading away.   **subject**   **predicate**

10. Wrinkled their noses.   **subject**   **predicate**

My score: ___
         10

My time: ....
              minutes   seconds

Minute 5

Name: .... **Date:** ....

Write the compound subject of each sentence on the line.

*(Hint: A **compound subject** is made up of two or more nouns or pronouns that share the same verb in the predicate.)*

1. My family and I went to Greece for our family holiday.

   ....

2. The beaches and shops were my favourite places to visit.

   ....

3. The roads and footpaths were very narrow.

   ....

4. The moon and the stars were very bright over the water.

   ....

5. Dad and Kevin played golf the day before we left.

   ....

6. The golf clubs and golf bag were a gift from my grandfather.

   ....

7. Mum and I sent my grandparents postcards and letters before we left.

   ....

8. Mum and Katie bought plenty of souvenirs for our friends.

   ....

9. The weather and people were very nice in Greece.

   ....

10. Spain or Italy is my choice for next year.

    ....

My score: $\dfrac{}{10}$

My time: ....
               minutes   seconds

Name: .... **Date:** ....

Circle the compound predicate in each sentence.

*(Hint: A **compound predicate** is made up of two or more verbs that share the same subject.)*

1. Bill was watching television and eating dinner.

2. Carla ran and skipped around the garden.

3. I drew and coloured the pictures.

4. The film was created and edited in one year.

5. The storm is damaging homes and moving closer to us.

6. Mum will wash and dry my old jacket.

7. John loved the book *Tomorrow, when the war began* and reread it many times.

8. We are removing the collage from the wall and taking it home.

9. The runner rested and relaxed after the race.

10. Frankie yawned and stretched after her long nap.

My score: ──── **My time:** ....
10   minutes   seconds

Name: ....   Date: ....

For Questions 1–10, circle yes if the sentence is declarative. Circle no if it is not.

*(Hint: A **declarative sentence** is a statement that tells about something.)*

1.	Career day at our school is finally here.	yes	no
2.	Mrs Smith, our class teacher, organised the event.	yes	no
3.	A veterinarian examined a hamster right in front of us!	yes	no
4.	Mandy wanted to speak with the police officers.	yes	no
5.	Is it possible to have more than one career?	yes	no
6.	I think I want to be a nurse or a scientist.	yes	no
7.	Our teacher said she once wanted to be a ballerina.	yes	no
8.	Now Mrs Smith is happy being a teacher.	yes	no
9.	Can we go and talk to the zookeeper?	yes	no
10.	Career day has helped me to decide to become a nurse.	yes	no

My score: ___ / 10

My time: ....
                 minutes   seconds

Minute 8

Name: .... **Date:** ....

For Questions 1–10, circle yes if the sentence is interrogative. Circle no if it is not.

*(Hint: An **interrogative sentence** is a question.)*

1. Will we take an aeroplane or a ferry to France? **yes**   **no**

2. We are going to visit my Aunt Mary and Uncle Mike. **yes**   **no**

3. Did you make sure to check the prices of a flight? **yes**   **no**

4. What day do you think we should leave? **yes**   **no**

5. How long are we going to visit them in France? **yes**   **no**

6. I hope we stay for a whole week! **yes**   **no**

7. They are my favourite aunt and uncle. **yes**   **no**

8. Do you remember the time we went on a picnic? **yes**   **no**

9. Did you like Uncle Mike's grilled chicken sandwiches? **yes**   **no**

10. We can visit them for Christmas next year, too. **yes**   **no**

My score: $\frac{}{10}$ **My time:** ....
                                        minutes   seconds

Name: .... Date: ....

Read the sentences below. Circle imperative *if the sentence is imperative*. Circle declarative *if it is declarative*.

*(Hint: An **imperative sentence** is a command. It ends with a full stop.)*

1. Please place the apples in the bowl on the table.	imperative	declarative
2. Stop playing your music so loud.	imperative	declarative
3. We had fun at the amusement park last weekend.	imperative	declarative
4. Make sure to purchase the tickets for the concert.	imperative	declarative
5. Marlon, you need to redo your assignment right now.	imperative	declarative
6. Jonathan sells raffle tickets to raise money for his scout group.	imperative	declarative
7. Tell me why you are not going to the school disco.	imperative	declarative
8. Give Justine one more chance to prove her point.	imperative	declarative
9. The doughnuts taste delicious.	imperative	declarative
10. Stop talking and listen to me.	imperative	declarative

My score: $\dfrac{}{10}$ My time: ....
                                                      minutes   seconds

Name: .... **Date:** ....

For Questions 1–10, circle yes if the sentence is exclamatory. Circle no if it is not.

(Hint: An **exclamatory sentence** shows strong feelings.)

1. Watch out for the deer crossing the street!   yes   no

2. You need to slow down!   yes   no

3. I am so glad the deer ran faster when they saw our car.   yes   no

4. We have seen a lot of farm animals today.   yes   no

5. Wow, that rabbit ran away just in time!   yes   no

6. Do you think we will see any more animals?   yes   no

7. Oh, look at the eagles flying above the car!   yes   no

8. Anna will be disappointed she didn't see the eagles.   yes   no

9. Oh my goodness, there goes another deer!   yes   no

10. This truly has been an amazing day!   yes   no

My score: _____

10

My time: ....
                                                    minutes   seconds

Name: .... **Date:** ....

For Questions 1–3, correct the run-on sentences by adding capital letters and punctuation marks in the appropriate places to make two complete sentences.

1. The Mississippi River runs through several states we took a boat ride along the Mississippi River.

2. Clara is a talented writer she writes in her journal daily.

3. We can exchange football cards I have plenty you would like.

For Questions 4–10, write yes if the sentence is a run-on. Write no of it is not.

4. Jessica forgot to tell Tina to water her plants while she was on holiday in Turkey.   ....

5. The rugby player scored several trys he is one of the best players on the team.   ....

6. Sandra and Wendy have lunch on Tuesday they like to eat Italian food.   ....

7. We did a great performance for the annual school Nativity.   ....

8. Clara hopes to write novels some day.   ....

9. It is nearly half past five we cannot reach town before dark.   ....

10. The sun is high put on some sunscreen.   ....

My score: _____
10

My time: ....
minutes   seconds

Minute 12

Name: ....   Date: ....

Read each group of words below. If the group of words is a complete sentence, circle sentence. If the group of words is not a complete sentence, circle fragment.

1. My favourite subject.   sentence   fragment

2. I really enjoy art, too, because we make collages.   sentence   fragment

3. In PE, I was the only one to run four laps.   sentence   fragment

4. Mario and Kenny.   sentence   fragment

5. I also like to eat lunch with my best friends.   sentence   fragment

6. After lunch we have science with Mrs Moyer.   sentence   fragment

7. We use a microscope with a lot of experiments.   sentence   fragment

8. In maths class.   sentence   fragment

9. In history class, we are studying the Ancient Egyptians. sentence   fragment

10. Reading the story of *The view from Saturday*.   sentence   fragment

My score: $\frac{}{10}$ My time: .... minutes   .... seconds

www.prim-ed.com   Prim-Ed Publishing®

Name: ....

Date: ....

Circle the subject in each sentence. Underline the predicate.

1. My mother has given my brother, my sister and me a list of chores today.

2. She has decided that now we need more responsibilities.

3. I have to clean out the garage.

4. Maggie and Josh have to dust all of the wooden furniture.

5. Josh has to trim the bushes around the garden.

6. Maggie and I will take a break after we wash the dishes.

7. Our dog, Coco, watches my sister and me make a snack.

8. Our father and mother have promised to take us to Pizza Place when we have finished.

9. My siblings and I are excited!

10. We quickly finish all of the chores.

My score:

$\dfrac{}{10}$

My time:

....
minutes   seconds

Name: .... **Date:** ....

For Questions 1–5, circle the compound subject.

1. The teacher and his pupils are excited that the class passed the test.

2. The dog and her puppies were protected from the storm.

3. The van and the car almost collided with each other on the busy road.

4. The cereal and toast were delicious.

5. Mum and I had dinner at that restaurant.

For Questions 6–10, add another subject.

6. Jerry and .... both had the flu last week.

7. The cool breezes and .... made the beach a perfect holiday spot.

8. Ed's hat and .... blew away in the wind.

9. My hamster and .... were my Christmas presents.

10. Joan and .... baked wholemeal raisin biscuits for their mum.

My score: $\frac{}{10}$

My time: ....
minutes   seconds

Name: ....   Date: ....

Circle the compound predicate in each sentence.

1. My brother and dad are mowing the lawn and raking the leaves.

2. Kourtney will vacuum the floors and empty the garbage.

3. Bobbi plants and waters the tulip bulbs in her garden.

4. Shawn sits and waits for his parents to pick him up from school.

5. The man thinks and wonders about his next step.

6. The singer danced around the stage and smiled at everyone.

7. My dog, Duke, barks and growls at the cat on the fence.

8. Martha cracks and stirs the eggs into the cake mix.

9. I spray and wipe the windows in my bedroom.

10. The little girl pouts and cries when she does not get her way.

My score: $\dfrac{}{10}$ **My time:** ....
minutes   seconds

Minute 16

Name: .... Date: ....

Read each sentence, and write the type of sentence it is on the line. Put **D** for declarative, **Int** for interrogative, **Imp** for imperative or **E** for exclamatory.

1. Megan learned how to horse ride this summer. ....

2. Sit up straighter on the horse. ....

3. Wow, I can't believe how fast she is going! ....

4. Can I take a picture of you and the horse? ....

5. I was so excited that Megan invited me to watch her practise! ....

6. The instructor offered to teach me as well. ....

7. I am going to ask my parents if I could take lessons. ....

8. I can't wait to learn to horse ride! ....

9. Let's go and eat lunch now. ....

10. I had so much fun spending time with Megan! ....

My score: $\dfrac{}{10}$

My time: ....
minutes   seconds

Name: .... Date: ....

For Questions 1–3, correct the run-on sentences by adding capital letters and punctuation marks in the appropriate places to make two complete sentences.

1. The floor is wet will you dry it so no-one falls?

2. We are going to the shopping centre many shops have sales.

3. Peter will not use the car today he will take the bus to get to work.

For Questions 4–10, write yes if the sentence is a run-on. Write no of it is not.

4. Yoko is excited to travel to Japan to visit her grandmother.   ....

5. She has not seen her grandmother in two years she was five years old the last time.   ....

6. Yoko's mother and sister will travel with her they will leave tomorrow.   ....

7. Her grandmother will meet them at the airport's baggage claim.   ....

8. This trip will be a nice chance for a family reunion.   ....

9. Yoko hopes there won't be any delays with travelling there are a few connecting fights.   ....

10. It can be quite tiresome having to wait at airports because of delayed flights.   ....

My score:

$\overline{10}$

My time:

....
minutes   seconds

Minute 18

Name: .... **Date:** ....

Circle the 10 nouns in the box. Write each noun in the table under the correct heading.

veterinarian	stir	meadow	smooth	paper bag
brave	souvenir	gallop	draw	courier
computer	brought	candle	theatre	creep
tennis court	gentle	dashing	runner	pleasant

Person	Place	Thing
1.	4.	7. ....
2.	5.	8. ....
3.	6.	9. ....
		10. ....

My score: $\dfrac{}{10}$ **My time:** ....

minutes   seconds

Prim-Ed Publishing®

www.prim-ed.com

Minute 19

Name: .... **Date:** ....

Circle the proper nouns in each sentence.

1. Harrison and George play baseball.

2. The name of their team is North Side Bears.

3. The boys really admire Coach Wesley.

4. He is from Cardiff in Wales.

5. Coach Wesley is a baseball coach for Moss Vale Secondary School.

6. Each Saturday he coaches the baseball team.

7. The games are on Sundays in October and November.

8. Mrs Wesley brings water and healthy snacks for the team.

9. If they win today's game, they will play against the Penrose Tigers.

10. The grand final will be held at Welby Playing Fields.

My score: $\frac{}{10}$ **My time:** ....
minutes   seconds

Name: .... **Date:** ....

Write each noun in the box under its correct category.

| building | Irish Sea | airport | Egypt | restaurant |
| Mount Everest | River Thames | Japan | actor | lampshade |

Common Nouns	Proper Nouns
1.	6. ....
2.	7. ....
3.	8. ....
4.	9. ....
5.	10. ....

My score: $\dfrac{}{10}$

My time: .... minutes .... seconds

Minute 21

Name: .... **Date:** ....

For Questions 1–10, write the plural form for each noun.

*(Hint: When a noun means more than one, it is **plural**. Plural nouns end in **–s**, **–es** or **–ies**.)*

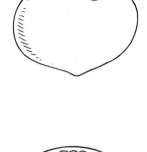

1. peach   ....

2. fox   ....

3. dress   ....

4. baby   ....

5. dish   ....

6. glass   ....

7. pineapple   ....

8. branch   ....

9. toy   ....

10. country   ....

My score: $\dfrac{}{10}$

My time: ....
                 minutes   seconds

Minute 22

Name: .... Date: ....

Circle the noun that best completes each sentence.

1. Did you know that certain (animal, animals) sleep during the day?

2. An (animal, animals) that sleeps during the day and is awake at night is nocturnal.

3. My (teacher, teachers), Ms Parker, did a lesson on nocturnal animals.

4. Kimberly and I were surprised that (skunk, skunks) are nocturnal.

5. Skunks eat insects and an occasional (rodent, rodents).

6. Skunks have long (claw, claws) that help them hunt.

7. Another nocturnal animal is a (toad, toads).

8. Toads have shorter (leg, legs) than frogs.

9. Toads hunt at night for food such as (insect, insects).

10. Next week our lesson will focus on (bat, bats).

My score: $\dfrac{}{10}$ **My time:** ....
                                        minutes   seconds

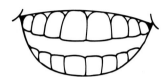

Name: .... **Date:** ....

For Questions 1–10, write the plural form for each noun.

*(Hint: Some nouns have unusual, or **irregular**, plurals. For example, if a noun ends with **–fe**, it is often necessary to change **f** to **v** and then add **–s** to make it plural.)*

1. life   ....

2. tooth   ....

3. goose   ....

4. leaf   ....

5. child   ....

6. hero   ....

7. person   ....

8. ox   ....

9. mouse   ....

10. scarf   ....

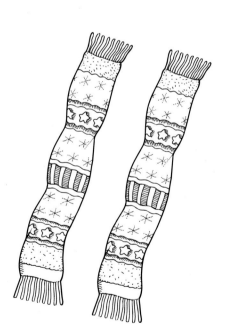

My score: ——————
            10

My time: ....
                    minutes   seconds

Name: .... **Date:** ....

Rewrite the underlined phrase in each sentence using a possessive noun.

1. The <u>tooth of the dog</u> was sharp. ....

2. The <u>pencils that belonged to Riley</u> were broken. ....

3. The <u>roof of the home</u> had leaks in ten places. ....

4. The <u>wings of the owl</u> were almost one metre long when extended. ....

5. The <u>flavour of the ice-cream</u> was strawberry. ....

6. The <u>tears on the jumper</u> came from the clothes hanger. ....

7. The <u>car that belonged to Luci</u> was damaged in the storm. ....

8. The <u>remote for the television</u> needed new batteries. ....

9. The <u>keys that belonged to Michele</u> were lost. ....

10. The <u>burgers from Happy Burger</u> are the best. ....

My score: $\frac{}{10}$

My time: ....
minutes   seconds

Minute 25

Name: .... **Date:** ....

Rewrite the underlined phrase in each sentence using a plural possessive noun.

1. The <u>parents of those girls</u> are famous actors.

....

2. The <u>uniforms of the soldiers</u> were filthy.

....

3. The <u>books the children borrowed</u> belong to the library.

....

4. The <u>bikes of the boys</u> are red and blue.

....

5. The <u>farm that my grandparents own</u> is located in South Australia.

....

6. The <u>toys of the dogs</u> are old and worn out.

....

7. The <u>faces of the models</u> were all very pretty.

....

8. The <u>eggs of the geese</u> were very safe from predators.

....

9. The <u>rafts of the men</u> were racing down the stream.

....

10. The <u>prey of the wolves</u> were hiding quietly.

....

My score: $\frac{\qquad}{10}$

My time: .... minutes .... seconds

Minute 26

Name: .... **Date:** ....

Use a subject pronoun from the box to replace the underlined words in each sentence. Write the pronoun on the line. (Some pronouns will be used more than once.)

(Hint: A **subject pronoun** takes the place of one or more nouns in the subject part of a sentence.)

you	he	she	it	we	they

1. <u>My family and I</u> will have a fantastic time on the camping trip.

   ....

2. <u>My parents</u> packed tents and sleeping bags into the van.

   ....

3. <u>My father</u> is looking forward to catching fish.

   ....

4. <u>My mother</u> brought pans and seasoning for cooking the fish.

   ....

5. <u>My brother and I</u> are putting up the tents.

   ....

6. <u>Shelby and Marisa</u> helped my mother clean the fish my dad caught.

   ....

7. <u>My piece of fish</u> was really tasty and fresh.

   ....

8. On Saturday <u>my family</u> went hiking in the forest.

   ....

9. <u>Frank</u> almost slipped off of a rock.

   ....

10. I know that <u>my friends</u> will enjoy a message about the trip.

    ....

My score: $\dfrac{\quad\quad}{10}$ **My time:** ....
minutes   seconds

Name: .... **Date:** ....

For Questions 1–5, circle the correct object pronoun to complete each sentence.

*(Hint: An **object pronoun** takes the place of one or more nouns in the action part of a sentence.)*

1. We enjoy making ice-cream sundaes and eating (it, them).

2. He sits near (I, me) in class.

3. She goes with (we, us) to the cinema a lot.

4. Nancy liked (she, her) very much.

5. I know (he, him) and his sister very well.

For Questions 6–10, write an object pronoun to complete each sentence.

6. Mark liked that watch and asked me to buy .... for his birthday.

7. I often go with both of .... to the city to shop and do errands.

8. The puppy at the pet store had a white spot on ....

9. Please make sure to give Robbie a hug when you see ....

10. The water was so cool and refreshing as I drank ....

My score: $\dfrac{}{10}$ **My time:** ....
minutes   seconds

Name: .... Date: ....

Circle the common nouns and underline the proper nouns in each sentence.

1. Mr Duncan just announced we are going to the High Museum.

2. We are going to take the bus there next Monday.

3. Our teacher said we would see paintings by Monet.

4. My mother has a Monet painting in our lounge.

5. Laci and I are excited because we also get to see ancient artefacts.

6. Unfortunately, we cannot take cameras to the museum.

7. Mrs Jones is going to come with us.

8. After we leave the museum, we are going to have lunch at Hyde Park.

9. Ahn and Staci have suggested we bring blankets to sit on.

10. The boys are going to bring a football to play with after we eat.

My score: $\dfrac{}{10}$ My time: ....
                                              minutes   seconds

Name: .... **Date:** ....

Circle the noun that correctly completes each sentence.

1. Tonya has a teddy (bear, bears) collection.

2. She has three (bear, bears) that are ten years old.

3. Tonya's favourite bear wears reading (glass, glasses).

4. Each bear in her collection is still in the (box, boxes) that it came in.

5. Her little (sister, sisters), Jenni, has tried to take them out of the boxes.

6. Their (mother, mothers) has scolded Jenni.

7. Tonya also has a few antique (doll, dolls) as well.

8. She has a (Barbie®, Barbies®) from the 1950s that her grandmother gave her.

9. Her grandmother also gave her a pair of antique (earring, earrings).

10. Tonya keeps them hidden in a little (case, cases) in her wardrobe.

My score: ___
10

My time: ....
minutes   seconds

Minute 30

Name: ....   Date: ....

For Questions 1-6, circle the correct irregular plural noun in each group of words below.

1.	loafs	loaves	loafes
2.	wolfs	wolves	wolfes
3.	children	childs	childrens
4.	lifeies	lives	lifes
5.	teethes	toothes	teeth
6.	women	womans	womanes

For Questions 7–10, write the irregular plural form for each noun.

7. cactus ....

8. sheep ....

9. knife ....

10. person ....

My score: ──── / 10

My time: ....
                minutes   seconds

Prim-Ed Publishing® www.prim-ed.com

Name: .... **Date:** ....

For Questions 1–10, make each phrase possessive.

1. light of the candle ....

2. uniforms of the children ....

3. pouch of the kangaroo ....

4. necklace of my mother ....

5. food of the calves ....

6. bibs of the netballers ....

7. car of the parents ....

8. picture of the girl ....

9. teacher of the pupils ....

10. trumpet of the bandleader ....

My score: $\dfrac{}{10}$ **My time:** ....
                                         minutes   seconds

Minute 32

Name: .... **Date:** ....

Rewrite the underlined phrase in each sentence using a pronoun.

1. The <u>princess</u> is wearing a beautiful dress to the ball.

   ....

2. She had <u>the dress</u> made by the best seamstress in the kingdom.

   ....

3. <u>Jackie and I</u> are going to help the princess prepare for the ball.

   ....

4. The princess hopes to dance with <u>the prince</u>.

   ....

5. <u>The prince</u> is visiting from another kingdom to meet the princess.

   ....

6. <u>The king and queen</u> are excited for their daughter.

   ....

7. <u>The king</u> wants the two kingdoms to join.

   ....

8. The princess rides in the carriage with <u>the king and queen</u>.

   ....

9. When they arrive at the ball, the prince is waiting for <u>the princess</u>.

   ....

10. <u>The prince</u> gives her a bouquet of roses.

   ....

My score: $\frac{}{10}$

My time: ....
   minutes   seconds

www.prim-ed.com   Prim-Ed Publishing®

Minute 33

Name: .... Date: ....

Find the verbs in the box and write them on the lines below.

pretty	destroy	lavender	breathe	slam
sister	migrate	studio	drag	collapse
smell	mattress	dive	dentist	trample
raincoat	build	dolphin	camera	bitter

1. ....

2. ....

3. ....

4. ....

5. ....

6. ....

7. ....

8. ....

9. ....

10. ....

My score: $\dfrac{}{10}$ **My time:** ....
minutes   seconds

Name: .... **Date:** ....

Circle the verbs in each sentence.

1. Keith snores very loudly.

2. The woman sneezed after she received a big bouquet of flowers.

3. The cat purred when Carla came into the room.

4. Bill bounces the ball on the court.

5. Susan strode her way to the finish line.

6. The fans cheered as the football star came onto the field.

7. We put our rubbish in the dustbin.

8. Can you see Bob smile at the camera?

9. My dog often barks at strangers.

10. The pigeons are perched outside my window.

My score: ——
10

My time: ....
minutes · seconds

Verb tense

Name: .... **Date:** ....

Circle the correct verb tense to complete each sentence.

1. My cousin, Holly, now (lived, lives) in New Zealand.

2. Her father once (owned, owns) a dog sled team.

3. Twice a year, the team (competes, competing) in a race.

4. This year my family is (travelling, travels) to New Zealand to see them compete.

5. Holly and I (sleeping, sleep) in her room.

6. She (helps, helping) her father prepare the dogs for the race.

7. I (watch, watching) from the window because I am scared of the dogs.

8. Uncle Joseph (reassures, reassuring) me that the dogs are nice.

9. During the race, we were all (waiting, waits) for my uncle to return.

10. He (won, winning) first place this year.

My score: $\dfrac{\rule{2cm}{0.4pt}}{10}$ **My time:** ....
minutes   seconds

Minute 36

Name: .... Date: ....

Write the past tense form of the verb in brackets to complete each sentence.

1. Jason (kick) .... the ball into the goal.

2. She (change) .... into her costume 30 minutes ago.

3. He (bow) .... after the audience gave him a standing ovation.

4. The magician (disappear) .... at the end of the magic show.

5. Carrie (greet) .... everyone at the door when they arrived.

6. The little girl (hurry) .... to catch the bus that was driving away.

7. The prince (kneel) .... down to kiss her hand.

8. I (measure) .... the milk before I poured it into the cake mixture.

9. We (observe) .... the life cycle of a tadpole last month in science.

10. Terry (promise) .... me he would do well in his exam.

My score: $\dfrac{}{10}$

My time: ....
            minutes   seconds

Name: .... **Date:** ....

For Questions 1–10, write yes if the verb is in the future tense or no if it is not.

1. I will perform in the ballet *The nutcracker* next year. ....

2. Are you ordering prawns or chicken? ....

3. I am going to scrub the kitchen floor tomorrow afternoon. ....

4. I will remember to cook the dinner tonight. ....

5. I will wash the clothes before I go to the restaurant. ....

6. Stop pretending you did not hear me! ....

7. I know she will listen to you when you call her later. ....

8. I included the directions in my letter. ....

9. I will develop a plan for the science project this evening. ....

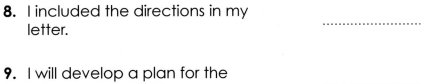

10. I had promised to clean my room when I got back. ....

My score: $\dfrac{}{10}$

My time: ....
minutes   seconds

Minute 38

Name: .... **Date:** ....

Complete the chart below by writing the correct verb form under each column.

Irregular verb	Past tense	Past participle *Hint: Past tense with a helping verb (**have**, **has**, **had**)*
1. drive	....	....
2. fly	....	....
3. begin	....	....
4. ride	....	....
5. ring	....	....
6. throw	....	....
7. write	....	....
8. tell	....	....
9. take	....	....
10. shake	....	....

My score: $\dfrac{}{10}$

My time: ....
minutes   seconds

Minute 39

Name: .... **Date:** ....

Write the correct form of the verb in brackets to complete each sentence.

1. I (admit) .... that I really like that colour on the wall.

2. We (applaud) .... when Diane received her award.

3. Gloria is (carry) .... the rose bouquet in the wedding.

4. Angus is (cheer) .... for the Everton Eagles to win.

5. The baby (cry) .... when his bottle fell to the floor.

6. I will always (disagree) .... with her statement.

7. I will (invite) .... Monica to the birthday dinner at our house.

8. I was (frighten) .... when the monster jumped in front of us at the haunted house.

9. Brenda (encourage) .... me to finish working on my science project.

10. I will (guess) .... the answer to the last question.

My score:
$\frac{}{10}$

My time: ....
minutes   seconds

Name: .... **Date:** ....

Use a linking verb from the box to complete each sentence. The words can be used more than once.

| are | seemed | is | were | am | was | feel | become | be |

1. Today will .... my first day in my new class.

2. I .... very nervous about meeting my new teacher each year.

3. Her name .... Mrs Robinson.

4. Mrs Robinson .... a trainee teacher last year.

5. Kate and Mei .... excited about the first day of school.

6. They .... up all night talking on the phone about their upcoming day.

7. When I met Mrs Robinson today, she .... pleasant.

8. Now I .... better knowing that she is a nice teacher.

9. Even though she assigned homework on the first day, I .... still excited.

10. My friends and I .... looking forward to the rest of the school year.

My score: $\dfrac{}{10}$ **My time:** ....
                                              minutes   seconds

Name: .... **Date:** ....

Use a helping verb from the box to best complete each sentence. The words can be used more than once.

| am | is | are | was | were | has | have | had | will |

1. The dog .... resting his head comfortably in his owner's lap.

2. Pam .... going to help us with the presentation yesterday before she became sick.

3. Tom and Louie .... solving the puzzle together when their mother called them.

4. I .... introducing the mayor at the banquet.

5. The man .... wandered for far too long.

6. Today we .... travel to Leeds for my sister's university graduation.

7. My grandfather and his friends .... sharing old war stories at the reunion.

8. Jane and Eve .... memorised their lines for the play.

9. We .... correcting the errors we made with the experiment.

10. She .... been sitting here in the waiting room for the doctor's appointment.

My score: ___
10

My time: ....
minutes   seconds

Minute 42

Name: .... **Date:** ....

For Questions 1–10, write your own verb that best completes each sentence.

1. The chef is .... a gourmet pasta dish.

2. He is .... fish to go with the pasta.

3. We will .... to the shops today to buy a gift for my aunt's birthday.

4. The man is .... a place to rest after his long journey.

5. Can you .... the key that I lost?

6. Edward will be .... in the race tomorrow.

7. Are you .... to the party after the cricket match?

8. I will .... my bike to the park with you.

9. The sun is .... brighter today than it was yesterday.

10. The pupils are .... clay pots in art class.

My score: $\dfrac{}{10}$

My time: ....
minutes   seconds

www.prim-ed.com   Prim-Ed Publishing®

Minute 43

Name: .... Date: ....

Complete the table below by writing the correct verb form under each column.

Verb	Present participle (Hint: Continuous action of a verb usually ending in -ing)	Past participle (Hint: Completed action described by a verb usually ending with -ed)
1. receive	....	....
2. destroy	....	....
3. plan	....	....
4. marry	....	....
5. sniff	....	....
6. sing	....	....
7. swim	....	....
8. carry	....	....
9. climb	....	....
10. taste	....	....

My score: $\frac{}{10}$

My time: ....
minutes   seconds

Name: .... **Date:** ....

Circle the correct verb form to complete each sentence.

1. The baby was (awoke, awakened) by the loud noise in the middle of the night.

2. Daniel (drew, drawn) an action hero for the art contest.

3. The children (run, ran) three laps before they played tennis.

4. Diane (sweep, swept) the kitchen floor after I washed the dishes.

5. I will (teach, taught) you how to ride a bike this summer.

6. It was (understand, understood) that he was not playing in the game.

7. The girl (weep, wept) when her parakeet suddenly flew away.

8. My mother (say, said) to come straight home after volleyball practice.

9. I (saw, seen) four films in one month.

10. Julie had (forget, forgotten) to water the plants last week.

My score: ___10___   **My time:** ....
                                              minutes   seconds

Name: .... Date: ....

Circle **yes** *if the sentence has the correct subject–verb agreement. Circle* **no** *if it is not. If the answer is* **no**, *write the correct verb on the line.*

1. Winston has many pairs of tennis shoes in his wardrobe.   yes   no   ....

2. Samantha and Allison make blueberry muffins for the cake sale.   yes   no   ....

3. The chicken sandwich tasted better once I added coleslaw dressing.   yes   no   ....

4. The thunder and lightening scare my dog last night.   yes   no   ....

5. I hope the tomatoes grows in my garden this year.   yes   no   ....

6. The tulips along the footpath are beautiful.   yes   no   ....

7. We is going to the rugby match to watch my brother play.   yes   no   ....

8. Brad fixed the broken window yesterday.   yes   no   ....

9. Today, Uncle Fred is arriving at the train station.   yes   no   ....

10. Ralph and Rachel are runs in the race today.   yes   no   ....

My score: $\frac{}{10}$

My time: ....
                         minutes   seconds

Name: ....   Date: ....

For each sentence, write whether the underlined word is a linking verb or a helping verb.

1. Tropical rainforests <u>are</u> located in places such as South America.

   ....

2. There <u>are</u> four layers of the rainforest.

   ....

3. The rainforest <u>is</u> usually wet because of the tropical climate.

   ....

4. Many animals <u>can</u> be found in the rainforest.

   ....

5. In class we <u>were</u> learning about the toucan and the vampire bat.

   ....

6. I <u>am</u> interested in knowing more about the king cobra.

   ....

7. The king cobra <u>is</u> located in the South-East Asian rainforests.

   ....

8. The king cobra <u>is</u> brown or black.

   ....

9. Mr Crenshaw <u>has</u> promised that we will learn more about cobras.

   ....

10. I guess I <u>could</u> do my own research about rainforest animals.

    ....

My score: ___
                 10

My time: ....
               minutes   seconds

Name: .... **Date:** ....

Circle the adjectives in the sentences below. Underline the noun that each adjective describes.

1. The bright girl did an excellent job on her project.

2. Rhonda bought four small apples from the markets on Saturday.

3. Unhappy Fran decided not to go to the party.

4. The day was dreadful because of all of the storms and hail.

5. The clumsy puppy fell over his huge feet as he ran.

6. The tall building is blocking my view of the park.

7. Sarah loves walking her dog in the park nearby.

8. My parents take us to the gourmet restaurant on Sundays.

9. Christian likes to eat chocolate ice-cream because it tastes delicious.

10. The water in the pool is very cold.

My score: $\dfrac{}{10}$

My time: ....
minutes seconds

Minute 48

Name: .... Date: ....

Complete the chart below by writing the correct form for each adjective.

Adjective	Comparative (Hint: adjectives that end in -er compare two nouns or pronouns)	Superlative (Hint: adjectives that end in -est compare more than two nouns or pronoun)
1. fast	....	....
2. great	....	....
3. soft	....	....
4. quick	....	....
5. slow	....	....
6. tall	....	....
7. low	....	....
8. clumsy	....	....
9. short	....	....
10. smooth	....	....

My score: —— / 10

My time: .... minutes .... seconds

www.prim-ed.com   Prim-Ed Publishing®

Minute 49

Name: .... **Date:** ....

Circle the adverb in each sentence. Underline the verb that the adverb describes.

*(Hint: An **adverb** is a word that describes a verb and tells **how**, **when** or **where** something happens.)*

1. The children excitedly put on their skates at the ice-skating rink.

2. The boys quickly dart to the rink before the girls.

3. The girls skate gracefully around the rink.

4. Mark bravely did a backwards flip in the centre of the rink.

5. The children happily clapped for Mark's performance.

6. The music softly played in the background.

7. The toddlers shrieked loudly as they skated around.

8. The beginner skaters carefully stepped onto the ice.

9. Some skaters wisely wore protective gear.

10. The more experienced skaters cautiously skated around the beginners.

My score: $\dfrac{\quad}{10}$ **My time:** ....

                                                        minutes   seconds

Minute 50

Name: .... **Date:** ....

For Questions 1–10, use the adverbs in the box to best complete each sentence.

nearby	forward	usually	never	after
now	somewhere	away	forever	late

1. I look .... to Christmas shopping every year.

2. My mother and I .... start our Christmas shopping after November.

3. We .... wait until the last minute, when the shops are crowded.

4. This year, we are going to shops that are ....

5. .... we have finished shopping, we have lunch at my family's restaurant.

6. We plan on going .... for our Christmas holidays.

7. It seemed as if I stood in a queue .... to post presents to my cousins.

8. My friends are going .... to visit relatives for their Christmas holidays.

9. The heavy traffic caused us to be .... for the New Year's party.

10. Let's choose our New Year's resolutions ....

My score: $\dfrac{}{10}$

My time: ....
minutes   seconds

www.prim-ed.com   Prim-Ed Publishing®

Name: .... **Date:** ....

For Questions 1–6, circle the word in each sentence that begins with a prefix.

1. Before I learned how to ride a bike, I first learned how to ride a tricycle.

2. I was very unhappy when my mother said I could not go to the cinema.

3. The swimming coach used a megaphone to yell instructions to the competition swimmers.

4. The famous singer gave me her autograph.

5. This afternoon, I am going to return my library books.

6. It was impossible to finish my book last night.

For Questions 7–10, circle the word that begins with a prefix.

7.	midnight	audience	minute
8.	tender	disappear	hundred
9.	blackbird	preview	bowler
10.	artistic	something	nonfiction

My score: $\dfrac{\quad\quad}{10}$

My time: ....
minutes   seconds

Minute 52

Name: ....   **Date:** ....

Add a suffix from the box to each word below. Write the new word on the line.

(Hint: A suffix is a group of letters that changes the meaning of a word when added to the end of it.)

able	er	ness	ish	ion	ful	ment	est	or	ship

1. child   ....

2. comfort   ....

3. wonder   ....

4. friend   ....

5. act   ....

6. govern   ....

7. kind   ....

8. protect   ....

9. teach   ....

10. smart   ....

My score: $\dfrac{}{10}$

My time: ....
                minutes   seconds

Minute 53

Name: .... **Date:** ....

For Questions 1–10, write yes if the commas are in the correct place or no if they are not.

*(Hint: A **comma** is a punctuation mark that is used to separate words in a list, to represent a slight pause in a sentence or to avoid confusion.)*

1. For Nick, Terrence was a hero. ....

2. York United, Kingdom ....

3. pens pencils, and paper ....

4. Sydney Melbourne and Canberra, ...

5. 18 Wattle Lane Hilton, Derby ....

6. Will, you Amyee do, that for me? ....

7. Rome, Italy ....

8. pickles, lettuce, onions, tomatoes and sauce ....

9. Paris France ....

10. Em, Amy Sean, Fran and Jess ....

My score: ──── $\frac{}{10}$

My time: ....
minutes   seconds

Name: ....   **Date:** ....

Insert the missing commas in each sentence.

1. Judy please make sure to buy a cake for Diane's birthday.

2. Even though it had been awhile I still remembered her phone number.

3. No I do not think it will rain today.

4. Because my favourite hobby is fishing my father gave me a new fishing rod.

5. The skinny furry puppy found a new home with Amy.

6. Yes I can start working on the science project next week.

7. Dita Karen and Lucy are going to make cream cheese and salmon sandwiches.

8. First Dita will take out a knife the cream cheese salmon and bread.

9. Next Karen will spread the cream cheese and place the salmon on the soft bread.

10. Last the girls will eat their sandwiches drink milk and play board games.

My score: $\dfrac{}{10}$ **My time:** ....
            minutes   seconds

Minute 55

Name: .... **Date:** ....

For Questions 1–10, change the words into abbreviations whenever possible and use initials for any first and middle names. (Don't forget the full stops, if necessary.)

1. Doctor Amber Jones ....

2. 23 August ....

3. William Christopher Handy ....

4. Second Street ....

5. Mister John Lewis Shaw ....

6. General Carol Elaine Barkley ....

7. 12 October ....

8. 12 Village Drive ....

9. Captain Douglas Harold Holmes ....

10. London, United KIngdom ....

My score: ___
10

My time: ....
minutes   seconds

Prim-Ed Publishing®   www.prim-ed.com

Grammar minutes   55

Minute 56

Name: .... Date: ....

For Questions 1–6, circle the adjectives in each sentence. Underline the nouns that the adjectives describe.

1. My beautiful mother makes the best chicken salad.

2. She uses smoked chicken that she grills on a hot fire.

3. My younger sister eats plenty of the tasty chicken salad sandwiches.

4. My older brother likes to take tiny bites to make it last longer.

5. My hardworking dad gets home too late to eat any of the delicious salad.

6. My caring mum decides to make more tasty salad for my dad.

Complete the table below by writing the correct form for each adjective in the columns.

Adjective	Comparative (Hint: adjectives that end in **-er** compare two nouns or pronouns)	Superlative (Hint: adjectives that end in **-est** compare more than two nouns or pronoun)
7. happy	....	....
8. scrawny	....	....
9. new	....	....
10. tricky	....	....

My score: $\dfrac{}{10}$

My time: ....
minutes   seconds

Prim-Ed Publishing® www.prim-ed.com

Name: .... **Date:** ....

Circle the adverb in each sentence. Underline the verb that the adverb describes.

1. The pupils observed the caterpillars closely.

2. The baker carefully removed the bread from the oven.

3. It rains often in the Amazon, Brazil.

4. The plane flew high above the storm clouds.

5. I rarely travel outside of my own country.

6. I finally understood why David was upset.

7. Kylie plays the xylophone well.

8. Raymond was terribly embarrassed when he tripped over his shoelaces.

9. Karen willingly discussed the incident with the police officer.

10. Today we read my favourite book by Ruth Park.

My score: $\dfrac{}{10}$

My time: ....
                minutes   seconds

Minute 58

Name: .... Date: ....

For Questions 1–10, circle prefix *if the word begins with a prefix. Circle* suffix *if the word ends with a suffix.*

1. disappear   **prefix**   **suffix**

2. flawless   **prefix**   **suffix**

3. thoughtful   **prefix**   **suffix**

4. illness   **prefix**   **suffix**

5. postpone   **prefix**   **suffix**

6. development   **prefix**   **suffix**

7. protection   **prefix**   **suffix**

8. nonchalant   **prefix**   **suffix**

9. reflect   **prefix**   **suffix**

10. prehistoric   **prefix**   **suffix**

My score: $\dfrac{}{10}$

My time: ....
          minutes   seconds

www.prim-ed.com   Prim-Ed Publishing®

Minute 59

Name: .... **Date:** ....

For Questions 1–10, write yes if the commas are in the correct place or no if they are not.

1. Jack, Tim Sam and Toby are on the football team with me. ....

2. Los, Angeles California ....

3. round, shiny cue ball ....

4. Kensington, London, England ....

5. Do you know the capital of Germany? ....

6. Maria, can you please bring me a piece of the pecan pie? ....

7. My sisters play baseball, hockey, netball and water polo. ....

8. 12 Pascal Way, Dublin Ireland ....

9. hard rough brown stick ....

10. Well, you shouldn't go to the park if you have homework to do. ....

My score: $\frac{}{10}$

My time: ....
          minutes   seconds

Name: ....   **Date:** ....

Rewrite the phrases below using abbreviations and or initials. (Don't forget the full stops, if required.)

1. also known as   ....

2. Doctor Trina Jackson   ....

3. 15 September   ....

4. Professor Snape   ....

5. United States of America   ....

6. British Broadcasting Corporation   ....

7. Miss Allison Cameron Peters   ....

8. Captain Hardaway   ....

9. Prime Minister Tuffin   ....

10. 17 December   ....

My score: $\frac{\quad}{10}$

My time: ....
minutes   seconds

Name: .... **Date:** ....

For Questions 1–4, draw lines to match two words to make a compound word.
Then write the word on the line.

1.   light   maker   ....

2.   team   drop   ....

3.   match   house   ....

4.   back   work   ....

For Questions 5–10, make compound words using the words in the box below. Use
each word only once.

down	fire	string	champion	ground	storm
fighter	ship	count	thunder	draw	fore

5. ....   6. ....

7. ....   8. ....

9. ....   10. ....

My score: $\dfrac{}{10}$ **My time:** ....
                                                         minutes   seconds

Name: .... **Date:** ....

For Questions 1–10, write the two words that make up each contraction on the lines.

1. should've

   ....

2. needn't

   ....

3. who'll

   ....

4. won't

   ....

5. let's

   ....

6. you're

   ....

7. doesn't

   ....

8. can't

   ....

9. could've

   ....

10. he'll

    ....

My score: $\dfrac{\quad}{10}$

My time: ....

minutes   seconds

Prim-Ed Publishing®

www.prim-ed.com

Minute 63

Name: .... Date: ....

Circle the synonym for each of the words in bold.

1. **build**   apart   construct   destroy

2. **speed**   haste   slow   shake

3. **move**   stop   transport   invite

4. **say**   remark   listen   watch

5. **timid**   unafraid   shy   obey

6. **slender**   thin   huge   nice

7. **awkward**   easy   clumsy   awake

8. **pain**   ache   lively   enough

9. **mistake**   correct   right   error

10. **depart**   early   leave   arrive

My score: $\frac{}{10}$

My time: ....
              minutes   seconds

Minute 64

Name: .... **Date:** ....

Circle the antonym for each of the words in bold.

1. **beautiful**	attractive	ugly	pretty
2. **empty**	bare	blank	full
3. **cruel**	friendly	brutal	vicious
4. **finish**	complete	begin	done
5. **different**	opposite	same	unlike
6. **individual**	together	single	solo
7. **active**	alive	inactive	busy
8. **freeze**	withhold	solidify	melt
9. **appear**	presence	disappear	seen
10. **speechless**	talkative	quiet	silent

My score: $\dfrac{}{10}$

My time: ....
minutes   seconds

Minute 65

Name: .... **Date:** ....

Circle the correct homophones to complete each sentence.

*(Hint: **Homophones** are words that sound the same but are spelt differently and have different meanings.)*

1. Please (meat, meet) me at the (meat, meet) counter in the supermarket.

2. The (principal, principle) at my school believes in the (principal, principle) of hard work.

3. Can you (buy, by) me some ice-cream at the shop (buy, by) the bookstore?

4. On (sundae, Sunday), the little girl had an ice-cream (sundae, Sunday).

5. I (knew, new) that my (knew, new) dress would be the prettiest at the ball.

6. The (rain, rein) on her horse snapped during the heavy (rain, rein).

7. The storm winds (blew, blue) the (blew, blue) plant pots over and smashed them.

8. The (made, maid) did her job around the house and also (made, maid) dinner.

9. My jersey ripped, (so, sew) my mum had to (so, sew) it for me before school.

10. I checked the (whether, weather) to help me decide (whether, weather) or not to bring a jacket with me.

My score: ___ /10   **My time:** .... minutes   .... seconds

Name: .... **Date:** ....

For each sentence, write yes if the underlined word is used correctly or no if it is not. If the answer is no, write the correct word on the second line.

1. Samuel is writing an essay <u>too</u> give to his teacher.

....

2. We may encounter the <u>two</u> hikers in the bush.

....

3. I love <u>to</u> go shopping with my mother and nanna.

....

4. It is <u>too</u> hot for the children to play at the beach.

....

5. Tim is the taller of the <u>to</u> boys.

....

6. I can use the library <u>to</u> practise my speech for the talk.

....

7. Will the rain ever reach <u>to</u> the top of the hill?

....

8. Aren't you using <u>two</u> much salt on the meat?

....

9. Ramsey will tell us where <u>to</u> go.

....

10. The light is <u>too</u> dim for the big ballroom.

....

My score: $\dfrac{}{10}$ **My time:** ....

minutes   seconds

Minute 67

Name: .... Date: ....

For Questions 1–5, write there, their *or* they're *to complete each sentence.*

1. .... were several places my family and I visited on our trip to South America.

2. My brother Kyle and sister Kay really enjoyed .... first trip to South America.

3. My parents were excited about going to Chile because they got

   married ....

4. .... are buses that go from country to country.

5. My parents said that .... going to buy tickets for the bus.

For Questions 6–10, circle the correct word to complete each sentence.

6. I studied Spanish before we left so I can speak some of it when I get (there, their, they're).

7. On the long aeroplane ride home, mum and Kay had to put earplugs in (there, their, they're) ears to sleep better.

8. The museum is over (there, their, they're) across the plaza.

9. (There, Their, They're) so excited to see all of the popular sights!

10. (There, Their, They're) trip was very exciting and relaxing as well.

My score: $\dfrac{}{10}$ **My time:** ....
                                              minutes   seconds

Minute 68

Name: .... **Date:** ....

For each sentence, write yes if the underlined word is used correctly or no if it is not. If the answer is no, write the correct word on the second line.

1. The bank is closing <u>you're</u> account.

    ....

2. Can you please stop <u>your</u> dog from barking!

    ....

3. The theatre near <u>you're</u> home burned down.

    ....

4. When you go to the museum, you will see <u>your</u> favourite painting.

    ....

5. <u>Your</u> going to love the new restaurant by the supermarket!

    ....

6. When you see <u>your</u> father, please give him this for me.

    ....

7. The clock will not stop on <u>your</u> command.

    ....

8. <u>Your</u> going to have the time of <u>your</u> life at the show.

    ....

9. We have to stay close to <u>you're</u> parents so we don't get lost.

    ....

10. Let's have <u>your</u> birthday party at the park.

    ....

My score: _____ / 10   **My time:** ....
minutes   seconds

www.prim-ed.com   Prim-Ed Publishing®

Name: .... **Date:** ....

Circle good *or* well *to complete each sentence.*

1. The man in the car accident is doing (well, good).

2. Sometimes my sister doesn't listen very (well, good).

3. Because of the sunny weather, it is a (well, good) day for a picnic.

4. Kane will choose a (well, good) spot for the picnic.

5. The tears from Belinda's eyes were not a (well, good) sign to see.

6. We will do a (well, good) job with washing and cleaning out your car.

7. Rodney is out of the hospital and is doing quite (well, good).

8. Stephanie did (well, good) at her dance recital.

9. The rocky road ice-cream tasted very (well, good).

10. I hope that your grandmother is doing (well, good).

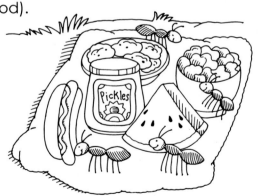

My score: $\dfrac{}{10}$

My time: ....
minutes   seconds

Name: .... **Date:** ....

Write affect *or* effect *to complete each sentence.*

*(Hint: **Affect** is almost always a verb; it means to influence or have an effect on. **Effect** is usually a noun; it means an outcome or result.)*

1. The weather tonight may .... whether or not we cancel the picnic.

2. The medicine I took for my cold had no .... on me.

3. My pocket money raise will take .... next week.

4. After I read the book, it seemed to .... the way I felt about the topic.

5. Rose did not let her low score for the test .... the great mood she was in.

6. The .... the sun had on my skin was obvious.

7. The pollution in the air can .... people's health.

8. The illness will only .... those who have not been vaccinated.

9. Not doing your homework will have an .... on your marks.

10. No matter how bad situations become, it shouldn't .... your attitude.

My score: $\dfrac{}{10}$ **My time:** ....
minutes   seconds

Minute 71

Name: .... **Date:** ....

Write accept *or* except *to complete each sentence.*

*(Hint: **Accept** is a verb that means 'to receive, admit, regard as true or say yes'. **Except** is often a preposition that means 'not including' or 'with the exception of'.)*

1. I will gladly .... the award on your behalf since you will be out of town.

2. I like most colours .... green and blue.

3. Jessica can do all swimming strokes .... the butterfly.

4. Paula will .... the apology from Ling.

5. I can go everywhere with you today .... for the last place.

6. All the pupils can go out to play .... Rick.

7. I can't .... this expensive gift.

8. He bought a gift for everyone .... me.

9. He will immediately .... the job.

10. I am going to .... the project even though it was late.

My score: _____
10

My time: ....
minutes   seconds

Name: .... **Date:** ....

Write a compound word to complete each sentence.

1. An insect that hops in the grass is a ....

2. A mate that you play with is a ....

3. A man that children can make out of snow is a ....

4. A bird that is black is a ....

5. A person who fights fire is a ....

6. A craft that flies in the air is an ....

7. A brush used to clean teeth is a ....

8. A chair that has wheels on it is a ....

9. A gown one would wear at night is a ....

10. A coat used when it is raining is a ....

My score: $\frac{}{10}$

My time: ....
minutes   seconds

Name: .... **Date:** ....

For Questions 1–10, circle the correct contraction in each group.

1.	I'd	i'd	ll'd
2.	are't	aren't	arne't
3.	the'll	they'l	they'll
4.	you've	youv'e	yo've
5.	woul'nd	would't	wouldn't
6.	musn't	must'nt	mustn't
7.	the're	they'r	they're
8.	doen't	doesn't	does'nt
9.	I'm	Im'	i'm
10.	is'nt	isn't	is'nt

My score: ——— / 10

My time: .... minutes .... seconds

Name: .... **Date:** ....

For each set of words, write **S** if the words are synonyms, write **A** if the words are antonyms or write **H** if the words are homophones.

1. every   entire   ....

2. damage   improve   ....

3. close   clothes   ....

4. destroy   create   ....

5. large   enormous   ....

6. fix   break   ....

7. better   worse   ....

8. ways   weighs   ....

9. grab   seize   ....

10. lone   loan   ....

My score: $\dfrac{}{10}$ **My time:** .... minutes   .... seconds

Minute 75

Name: .... Date: ....

For each sentence, write yes if the underlined word is used correctly or no if it is not. If the answer is no, write the correct word on the second line.

1. My parents like art, and they're favourite artist is Leonardo DaVinci.

   ....

2. Leonardo has two famous paintings that my mother loves.

   ....

3. There names are the *Mona Lisa* and *The Last Supper*.

   ....

4. To bad the originals are not for sale.

   ....

5. However, they're available as posters in museum gift shops.

   ....

6. I hope one day my paintings will be in your museum.

   ....

7. You have to bring you're passports when you travel to New York.

   ....

8. The museums there are known for the famous artworks that are displayed.

   ....

9. How about we go too the park and have a picnic afterwards?

   ....

10. Their going to go on another trip next year.

   ....

My score: ___ / 10

My time: ....
minutes   seconds

Minute 76

Word usage – review: *good* or *well*

Name: .... **Date:** ....

For Questions 1–10, write **good** *or* **well** *in the blank to complete each sentence.*

1. Today is a .... day to go fishing with my cousin Anthony.

2. I called him, but his mother said he was not feeling ....

3. My Aunt Gina also didn't feel .... that morning.

4. I was disappointed because I am not .... at catching fish.

5. The last time we went fishing, Anthony did a .... job of catching fish.

6. I cleaned the fish ...., and our entire family had homemade fish and chips.

7. I'm going to need a .... night's rest after the long day.

8. I didn't sleep very .... last night since I was so excited for the fishing trip.

9. Even though I didn't catch any fish, I had a .... time.

10. The day was .... worth the drive to the lake.

My score: $\dfrac{}{10}$

My time: .... minutes .... seconds

www.prim-ed.com Prim-Ed Publishing®

Minute 77

Name: .... **Date:** ....

For Questions 1–10, circle the word that correctly completes each sentence.

1. With the lack of sleep, your performance will be (affected, effected).

2. The evacuation will be in (affect, effect) tonight.

3. I will have to (accept, except) the offer for help.

4. I would help you, (accept, except) I'm too busy.

5. The (affect, effect) of the glare from the sun caused the car accident.

6. She finally (accepted, excepted) the fact that her lost dog is not coming home.

7. I can play most sports (accept, except) for tennis and golf.

8. The use of mobile phones may (effect, affect) the brain and cause tumours.

9. Mrs Whitley will not (accept, except) any late history projects.

10. The medicine had an immediate (effect, affect) on my headache.

My score: ____/10   **My time:** ....
minutes   seconds

Minute 78

Name: .... Date: ....

For Questions 1–6, write lose or loose *to complete each sentence.*

*(Hint: **Lose** is a verb that means to suffer the loss of. **Loose** is an adjective that means the opposite of tight or contained.)*

1. Margo will .... her keys if she keeps them in her big pockets.

2. A .... wire is the reason why my car radio will not work.

3. I have a lot of .... change at the bottom of my purse.

4. You are going to .... that dog if you do not keep him on a leash.

5. Our team is going to .... the match if we do not score one more goal.

6. My little brother has two .... teeth on the bottom row.

For Questions 7–10, write yes *if the underlined word is used correctly. Write* no *if it is not.*

7. My mother has decided to eat healthily and exercise to <u>lose</u> some weight.   ....

8. Her ponytail came <u>lose</u> when she ran in the all-star race.   ....

9. The skirt was <u>loose</u> around my waist, but I bought it anyway.   ....

10. If we do not play well in the second half, we will <u>lose</u> the match.   ....

My score: ____ / 10

My time: .... minutes .... seconds

Name: .... Date: ....

Write *chose* or *choose* *to complete each sentence.*

*(Hint: Use **chose** for past tense and **choose** for present tense.)*

1. Miley .... to stay at home instead of going to Byron Bay with her friends.

2. Please hurry up and .... the pair of jeans you are going to wear.

3. I really hope Kelly will .... me to be on her team for the debate next week.

4. Jason .... to fly to the sports event instead of taking a train.

5. The teacher will .... five pupils to be in the school play.

6. Lucy .... to have pizza last night instead of kebabs.

7. I think I will .... this pair of shoes because they are comfortable.

8. The dog .... to stay outside in the rain instead of going into his kennel.

9. I .... the red jacket instead of the blue one.

10. I will have to .... the best shirt to wear to my aunt's wedding.

My score: $\frac{}{10}$

My time: ....
minutes   seconds

Minute 80

Name: .... Date: ....

Write its *or* it's *to complete each sentence.*

*(Hint: **Its** is the possessive form of 'it'. **It's** is a contraction of 'it is' or 'it has'.)*

1. The eagle soared above .... nest in the gorge.

2. .... not often that we go on picnics together.

3. My brother always has football practices and .... important that he is there.

4. I have ballet rehearsal four days a week and .... very tiring at times.

5. Today my mother is packing our lunch for the picnic and .... going to be delicious!

6. The cat fell asleep in .... cosy bed.

7. .... great to be able to spend time with my family.

8. When it is hot outside, the dog naps in .... hiding place under the bush.

9. A happy dog wags .... tail.

10. I'm so excited because .... almost my birthday!

My score: $\frac{}{10}$

My time: ....
minutes   seconds

www.prim-ed.com   Prim-Ed Publishing®

Minute 81

Name: .... **Date:** ....

Write yes if than or then is used correctly. Write no if it is not.

*(Hint: **Than** is used in a sentence when comparing two things. **Then** describes a point in time.)*

1. Carla likes jazz better <u>than</u> classical music. ....

2. Simone is going to the shopping centre and <u>then</u> the cinema with Jeff. ....

3. If you are going with us, <u>than</u> you need to hurry and get dressed. ....

4. I prefer to scuba dive <u>than</u> surf when we go to the beach. ....

5. Huan would rather do his homework <u>than</u> wash dishes. ....

6. Tony will wash his car and <u>then</u> clean out his garage. ....

7. Leona and her mother will bake biscuits and <u>than</u> cook dinner. ....

8. Kevin dances much better <u>then</u> me. ....

9. Ashley and Dan would rather go to the rugby finals <u>then</u> watch it at home. ....

10. Mexico has whiter beaches <u>than</u> Tenerife. ....

My score: $\dfrac{}{10}$ **My time:** ....
   minutes   seconds

Minute 82

Name: .... Date: ....

For Questions 1–10, choose a word from the box to best complete each sentence. The words may be used more than once.

never	no	not	nobody
nothing	nowhere	none	neither

1. I had .... cheesecake nor chocolate cake.

2. We are going .... near the Tiwi Islands because of the cyclone.

3. I have .... seen the new film with my favourite actor and actress.

4. .... will come to your party if you continue to act mean to them.

5. ...., I cannot keep giving you money to buy junk food!

6. Trisha wanted a piece of cake, but there was .... left.

7. There was .... in the pantry but a box of crackers and a jar of strawberry jam.

8. I would .... go skydiving out of a plane!

9. .... of the children want to take a nap.

10. The keys were .... to be found.

My score: ____ / 10   My time: .... minutes   .... seconds

Name: .... **Date:** ....

For Questions 1–5, write yes if the article is used correctly. Write no if it is not. If the answer is no, write the correct word on the second line.

1. Can we read a book *The wizard of Rondo*?

   ....

2. A squirrel walked in front of us on our hike through the forest.

   ....

3. The purpose of this meeting is to decide on the topic of our project.

   ....

4. The Thai salad would taste even better if you add a onion.

   ....

5. Kevin found a lost dog that everyone was looking for.

   ....

For Questions 6–10, circle the correct article to complete each sentence.

6. After (an, the) match on Friday, we went for ice-cream.

7. We had ice-cream at (a, an) ice-cream shop by the market.

8. I ordered vanilla ice-cream with peanuts, caramel and (the, a) cherry.

9. My sister had (a, the) banana split with lots of whipped cream.

10. I saw some of my friends at (an, the) ice-cream shop as well.

My score: $\dfrac{}{10}$

My time: ....
minutes   seconds

Name: .... Date: ....

Choose a preposition or prepositional phrase from the box to best complete each sentence below.

together with	about	after	instead of	in
between	by	of	behind	into

1. Today my teacher announced we were going to read a book
.... a pig and a spider.

2. The title .... the book is *Charlotte's web*.

3. My mother and I went to a bookshop .... school to purchase the book.

4. At first we did not see any copies, but luckily we found one
.... another book.

5. My mother read magazines .... looking around the shop with me.

6. I ran .... my best friend, Katie, at the bookshop.

7. .... Katie, I shopped for more books.

8. .... the two of us, we bought six books to add to our collections.

9. .... the time we were done, the shop was closing.

10. My mother was already standing .... the queue with her magazines.

My score: $\frac{}{10}$

My time: ....
minutes   seconds

Prim-Ed Publishing®
www.prim-ed.com

Minute 85

Name: .... **Date:** ....

For Questions 1–4, circle the correct word to complete each sentence.

1. You will (lose, loose) your keys if you are not careful.

2. Her shoelaces came (lose, loose) when she was running the race.

3. I will (chose, choose) my team members for the debate.

4. I (chose, choose) to go to the greengrocer instead of the farmers' market.

For Questions 5–10, write lose, loose, chose or choose to best complete each sentence.

5. I am trying to .... whether to play netball or hockey.

6. If you keep wearing trousers with holes in the pocket, you may .... your wallet.

7. His shoelaces were .... during the race, causing him to trip and fall.

8. Gary .... to stay at home instead of going to the theatre.

9. Hannah did not ....any teeth until the age of seven.

10. Paul .... to wash his dog this morning instead of this evening.

My score: $\frac{}{10}$ **My time:** ....
                                              minutes   seconds

Name: .... **Date:** ....

For Questions 1–5, write than _or_ then _to complete each sentence._

1. Elise watched the shooting star and .... made a wish.

2. Gail will eat lunch and .... go shopping with her mother for new clothes.

3. I think I would rather run .... join the swimming team this school year.

4. We broke the door hinge when we opened it farther .... it was supposed to go.

5. The new teacher is more patient with the pupils .... the old teacher was.

For Questions 6–10, write its _or_ it's _to complete each sentence._

6. .... a great day to go swimming in my pool.

7. I think I will wear my pink and green swimsuit with .... matching sunhat.

8. My mother said .... not a good idea for me to do a flip off the diving board.

9. The diving board isn't hanging properly because .... missing a few screws.

10. The dog licked .... paws after it came inside.

My score: $\dfrac{}{10}$ **My time:** .... minutes seconds

Name: .... Date: ....

Write yes if the underlined words are used correctly. Write no if it is not.

1. I barely had <u>no</u> money left over to buy the cupcakes.　　............................

2. Sean <u>doesn't</u> have invitations left to give out for his party.　　............................

3. Darby could find <u>nowhere</u> to park at the supermarket.　　............................

4. Chris hardly has <u>no</u> experience as a firefighter.　　............................

5. I don't have <u>nobody</u> to watch my dog while I am out of town.　　............................

For Questions 6–10, choose a word from the box to best complete each sentence.

scarcely	no-one	barely	not	hardly

6. Claudia .... had enough time to write her research paper on Nina Simone.

7. She was .... able to find her biography at the bookshop.

8. Her dad could .... afford to buy the rare jazz albums for his collection.

9. Luckily, her mother put the recordings away so .... could break them.

10. At her presentation, Claudia .... made a mistake and received a perfect score.

My score: $\frac{}{10}$　　**My time:** ....
　　　　　　　　　　　　　　　　　　　　minutes　　　seconds

Minute 88

Name: .... Date: ....

Write the correct article (a, an) for each word.

1. .... village

2. .... adult

3. .... child

4. .... prawn

5. .... amateur

6. .... estimate

7. .... necklace

8. .... island

9. .... anniversary

10. .... map

My score: $\frac{}{10}$

My time: ....
minutes   seconds

Minute 89

Name: .... **Date:** ....

Circle the correct preposition or prepositional phrase to complete each sentence.

1. (Without, Within) prior knowledge, I was still able to give an acceptance speech.

2. Darcy finally was able to stop working (on, of) her project and take a break.

3. Please put the dog (out, off) while we paint the kitchen.

4. We are going to the amusement park (at, on) the weekend.

5. (Because of, Close to) the rain, the outdoor cinema is closed.

6. The new doughnut shop is (near, next) to the hairdressers.

7. The biscuit jar is on the shelf (above, upon) the toaster.

8. My favourite book was written (by, in) Chris Van Burg.

9. I sat (next to, above) Joan on the aeroplane.

10. The hawk flew high (over, beneath) the trees in the forest.

My score: $\dfrac{}{10}$

My time: ....
            minutes   seconds

Apply your grammar knowledge

Name: .... **Date:** ....

Write what the sentence is missing on the line. Put N for noun, V for verb, P for preposition or A for adjective.

1. Polar bears are found .... the Arctic Ocean.

2. Male polar bears .... around 350 to 650 kilograms.

3. A polar bear's diet consists of seals, ... and kelp.

4. Their .... fur keeps them warm in the cold temperatures.

5. Polar bears have .... paws that help them swim well.

6. They do not hibernate like other ....

7. The roller-coaster was a scary ride .... the amusement park.

8. The River Nile is one of the .... rivers in the world.

9. The summer reading list will be .... on the board.

10. His informal .... did not match his black pinstripe suit.

My score: ___ / 10

My time: ....
minutes   seconds

Minute 91

Name: ....   **Date:** ....

*Write yes if the group of words is a complete sentence. Write **no** if it is not.*

1. Not going to the library tomorrow. ....

2. Will you please keep my hamsters while I am on holiday? ....

3. Timothy, the ball. ....

4. Are great pets to own. ....

5. Sweets are not always good to eat because they can cause cavities. ....

6. We will be moving the furniture to the new house tomorrow. ....

7. Giggled when the clown came out of the cake. ....

8. Can you help me with face painting at my sister's party? ....

9. Flying kites at the park on a sunny day. ....

10. Rebecca forgot to tell her mother about the school trip to the museum. ....

My score: $\frac{}{10}$ **My time:** ....
                                              minutes   seconds

Minute 92

Name: .... **Date:** ....

Circle the misused word in each sentence. Write the correct word on the line.

1. After the rain, their was a lot of mud in my garden. ....

2. Mitch and Bill miss the grand final last night. ....

3. I doesn't know why the lights keep blinking off and on. ....

4. There are to apples left in the bowl to make a fruit salad. ....

5. I like most vegetables accept tomatoes and carrots. ....

6. The storm clouds covered the blew sky before the cyclone. ....

7. You're science project will probably win first place. ....

8. Angus seen his new dirt bike in the garage. ....

9. Greg maid sure to study for his history test. ....

10. I won't to be a detective for a secret agency when I grow up. ....

My score: $\dfrac{}{10}$ **My time:** ....

minutes   seconds

Name: .... **Date:** ....

If the sentence has a compound subject, write CS. If the sentence has a compound predicate, write CP.

1. The tyres and bell on my bicycle need to be replaced. ....

2. Sunrise and sunset are my favourite sights to watch. ....

3. My father sanded down and painted my old wooden desk. ....

4. Our tour and holiday were cut short because of the storm. ....

5. The coach instructs and guides the team during the warm-up. ....

6. Chloe ran and screamed as the dog growled at her through the fence. ....

7. Jacob and his sister caught butterflies on their camping trip. ....

8. My teacher and my parents were proud of me for gaining top marks. ....

9. The boys were running and jumping in the snow on the playground. ....

10. I was smiling and laughing uncontrollably at his funny jokes. ....

My score: $\dfrac{\quad}{10}$

My time: ....
minutes   seconds

Name: .... **Date:** ....

For Questions 1–6, circle the misused word in each sentence. Write the correct word on the line.

1. Oscar did quite good on his maths test considering he did not study.

   ....

2. Even though the idea was a good one, its not going to work for us.

   ....

3. Their is a great chance that there will be a flood next week.

   ....

4. She flower girl dress for the wedding was pink with a satin bow.

   ....

5. A elevator was stuck for two hours in the Dalton Building.

   ....

6. Him father is teaching him how to play golf.

   ....

For Questions 7–10, correct each sentence with capital letters and punctuation.

7. gina bought the doughnuts from mr smiths doughnut shop

8. We moved to london england from madrid spain

9. May we go to mount buffalo national park on saturday

10. mrs brock was my favourite teacher at gawler primary school

My score: $\frac{}{10}$

My time: ....
minutes   seconds

Apply your grammar knowledge

Name: .... **Date:** ....

For Questions 1–4, if the group of words is a sentence write S. If the group of words is a fragment, write F.

1. My new shoes. ....

2. Mindy could not go to the circus because she had the flu. ....

3. The house on the hill. ....

4. Kept me awake last night. ....

For Questions 5–10, circle the correct word to complete each sentence.

5. The baby will (ball, bawl) if you take his (ball, bawl) away from him.

6. The pupil looked at the (bored, board) with a (bored, board) look on his face.

7. We will stay (inn, in) the Lakeside (inn, in) as soon as the rest of our family arrives.

8. The brave (knight, night) rode his horse into the (knight, night).

9. The pupils need to (right, write) their reports (right, write) away.

10. She had to (wait, weight) for her turn to use the (wait, weight) machine at the gym.

My score: $\frac{}{10}$

My time: ....
minutes   seconds

Name: .... Date: ....

For Questions 1–6, rewrite the underlined phrase in each sentence using the correct pronoun.

1. <u>Lisa and Wendy</u> were surprised when their sculpture won first place.

   ....

2. <u>Oliver and I</u> tried to be on time for the party, but we were late.

   ....

3. <u>Linda</u> was not happy when she found out that her dog ran away.

   ....

4. <u>Jason</u> watched in awe as the butterfly emerged from the chrysalis.

   ....

5. Meg planted flowers in <u>her parents'</u> garden.

   ....

6. The tiger chased <u>the boar</u> into the jungle.

   ....

For Questions 7–10, circle whether the sentence is declarative, interrogative, imperative or exclamatory.

7. Stand over there and I will take your picture.

   declarative   *interrogative*   *imperative*   *exclamatory*

8. What would you like to have for dinner?

   declarative   *interrogative*   *imperative*   *exclamatory*

9. We are going ice-skating on Saturday.

   declarative   *interrogative*   *imperative*   *exclamatory*

10. I am so excited for the surprise party!

    declarative   *interrogative*   *imperative*   *exclamatory*

My score: ___/10   My time: .... minutes .... seconds

www.prim-ed.com   Prim-Ed Publishing®

Apply your grammar knowledge

Name: .... **Date:** ....

For Questions 1–5, circle the noun form that correctly completes each sentence.

1. The hottest (desert, deserts) in the world is the Sahara.

2. The Sahara has some rivers and (stream, streams) running through it.

3. The most famous (river, rivers) is the River Nile.

4. Even though it barely rains, when it does (rain, rains), it can last for hours.

5. The desert is home to many (animals, animal), including lizards and snakes.

For Questions 6–10, circle **linking** *if the underlined word is a linking verb or circle* **helping** *if it is a helping verb.*

6. The trip to the ocean <u>was</u> peaceful.	**linking**	**helping**
7. My baby sister <u>is</u> five years old.	**linking**	**helping**
8. The Johnsons <u>are</u> driving to their grandparents' home.	**linking**	**helping**
9. Sarah <u>was</u> sad when her dog ran away.	**linking**	**helping**
10. I <u>should</u> carry the heavy box for my sister.	**linking**	**helping**

My score: $\frac{}{10}$

My time: ....
minutes   seconds

Name: .... **Date:** ....

Circle the correct verb form to complete each sentence.

1. The little girl (pout, pouted) when she could not have her way.

2. Please do not (snatches, snatch) that from me!

3. The dog (glaring, glared) at the cat that was hiding in the tree.

4. The soldiers will (march, marched) in the parade tomorrow.

5. The (shrieking, shriek) animal scared us on the nature trail.

6. The baby (clung, clinging) to his mother when she picked him up.

7. We were able to (dodge, dodging) the truck that swerved into our lane.

8. I (wincing, winced) when my mother cleaned the cut on my finger.

9. Mary gave a low (chuckles, chuckle) when the cartoon cat tripped.

10. Phil (hums, hummed) along with the song before he played it on his trumpet.

My score: —— **My time:** ....

$\frac{}{10}$

minutes   seconds

www.prim-ed.com   Prim-Ed Publishing®

Minute 99

Name: .... **Date:** ....

For Questions 1–6, use the words in the box to make compound words. Use each word only once.

1. ....

2. ....

3. ....

4. ....

5. ....

6. ....

no	room
spot	shelf
lip	ever
how	light
ball	body
book	stick

For Questions 7–10, write yes if the underlined word is used correctly. Write no if it is not.

7. She <u>chose</u> to stay home instead of going on the trip to the Blue Mountains. ....

8. The speech will have an <u>effect</u> on your opinion of the candidate. ....

9. I have to <u>accept</u> the cancellation of the car warranty. ....

10. The little girl's tooth is <u>loose</u>. ....

My score: —— / 10

My time: .... minutes .... seconds

Name: .... **Date:** ....

For Questions 1–5, circle yes if the sentence has the correct subject-verb agreement. Circle no if it does not. If the answer is no, write the correct verb on the line.

1. Joey taken the bus to the shopping centre to buy a Christmas gift. yes no ....

2. The two singers waited impatiently to hear who won the contest. yes no ....

3. Justin and Hazel were having fun rollerskating with their friends. yes no ....

4. Susie discuss the idea with her parents. yes no ....

5. Gary makes homemade muffins for my party last night. yes no ....

For Questions 6–10, correct each sentence by adding all of the missing punctuation marks.

6. If Maggie calls tell her to come an hour earlier

7. Jackson can play the drums the tambourine the flute and the guitar

8. May we eat dinner go to the cinema go bowling and perhaps play pool

9. Hira please don't forget to put the potato salad in the fridge

10. Watch out for the dog crossing the road

My score: $\dfrac{}{10}$ **My time:** ....
minutes   seconds

Prim-Ed Publishing®
www.prim-ed.com

Minute answer key

Minute 1
1. sentence
2. fragment
3. sentence
4. sentence
5. sentence
6. fragment
7. sentence
8. fragment
9. fragment
10. sentence

Minute 2
1. We
2. Flamingos
3. Some people
4. Kyra
5. The zookeeper
6. Judy
7. Our teacher
8. Female flamingos
9. Baby flamingos
10. Our class

Minute 3
1. prepares for our first game
2. demonstrates how to dribble the ball correctly
3. blocked the ball from going into the basket
4. were practising their free throws
5. showed us how to block the offence
6. scored a three-pointer right before the buzzer went off
7. were also practising in the gym
8. is the captain of the cheerleading squad
9. run laps around the gym to strengthen our legs
10. is ready for the game on Friday

Minute 4
1. predicate
2. subject
3. predicate
4. predicate
5. subject
6. subject
7. subject
8. predicate
9. subject
10. subject

Minute 5
1. My family and I
2. The beaches and shops
3. The roads and footpaths
4. The moon and the stars
5. Dad and Kevin
6. The golf clubs and golf bag
7. Mum and I
8. Mum and Katie
9. The weather and people
10. Darwin or the Kimberley

Minute 6
1. was watching television and eating dinner
2. ran and skipped around the garden
3. drew and coloured the pictures
4. was created and edited in one year
5. is damaging homes and moving closer to us
6. will wash and dry my old jacket
7. loved the book *Tomorrow, when the war began* and reread it many times
8. are removing the collage from the wall and taking it home
9. rested and relaxed after the race
10. yawned and stretched after her long nap

Minute 7
1. yes
2. yes
3. no
4. yes
5. no
6. yes
7. yes
8. yes
9. no
10. yes

Minute 8
1. yes
2. no
3. yes
4. yes
5. yes
6. no
7. no
8. yes
9. yes
10. no

Minute 9
1. imperative
2. imperative
3. declarative
4. imperative
5. imperative
6. declarative
7. imperative
8. imperative
9. declarative
10. imperative

Minute 10
1. yes
2. yes
3. no
4. no
5. yes
6. no
7. yes
8. no
9. yes
10. yes

Minute 11
1. The Mississippi River runs through several states. We took a boat ride along the Mississippi River.
2. Clara is a very talented writer. She writes in her journal daily.
3. We can exchange football cards. I have plenty you would like.
4. no
5. yes
6. yes
7. no
8. no
9. yes
10. yes

Minute 12
1. fragment
2. sentence
3. sentence
4. fragment
5. sentence
6. sentence
7. sentence
8. fragment
9. sentence
10. fragment

Minute 13
1. subject: My mother; predicate: has given my brother, my sister and me a list of chores today
2. subject: She; predicate: has decided that now we need more responsibilities
3. subject: I; predicate: have to clean out the garage
4. subject: Maggie and Josh; predicate: have to dust all of the wooden furniture
5. subject: Josh; predicate: has to trim the bushes around the garden
6. subject: Maggie and I; predicate: will take a break after we wash the dishes
7. subject: Our dog, Coco; predicate: watches my sister and me make a snack
8. subject: Our father and mother; predicate: have promised to take us to Pizza Place when we have finished
9. subject: My siblings and I; predicate: are excited
10. subject: We; predicate: quickly finish all of the chores

Minute 14
1. The teacher and his pupils
2. The dog and her puppies
3. The van and the car
4. The cereal and toast
5. Mum and I
6–10. Answers will vary.

Minute 15
1. are mowing the lawn and raking the leaves
2. will vacuum the floors and empty the garbage
3. plants and waters the tulip bulbs in her garden
4. sits and waits for his parents to pick him up from school
5. thinks and wonders about his next step
6. danced around the stage and smiled at everyone
7. barks and growls at the cat on the fence
8. cracks and stirs the eggs into the cake mix
9. spray and wipe the windows in my bedroom
10. pouts and cries when she does not get her way

Minute 16
1. D
2. Imp
3. E
4. Int
5. E
6. D
7. D
8. E
9. Imp
10. E

Minute 17
1. The floor is wet. Will you dry it so no-one falls?
2. We are going to the shopping centre. Many shops have sales.

Minute answer key

3. Peter will not use the car today. He will take the bus to get to work.
4. no
5. yes
6. yes
7. no
8. no
9. yes
10. no

Minute 18

Answers may be in any order.

1–3. veterinarian
runner
courier
4–6. tennis court
meadow
theatre
7–10. souvenir
candle
computer
paper bag

Minute 19

1. Harrison, George
2. North Side Bears
3. Coach Wesley
4. Cardiff, Wales
5. Coach Wesley, Moss Vale Secondary School
6. Saturday
7. Sundays, October, November
8. Mrs Wesley
9. Penrose Tigers
10. Welby Playing Fields

Minute 20

Answers may be in any order.

1–5. building
airport
restaurant
lampshade
actor
6–10. Irish Sea
Egypt
Mount Everest
Japan
River Thames

Minute 21

1. peaches
2. foxes
3. dresses
4. babies
5. dishes
6. glasses
7. pineapples
8. branches
9. toys
10. countries

Minute 22

1. animals
2. animal
3. teacher

4. skunks
5. rodent
6. claws
7. toad
8. legs
9. insects
10. bats

Minute 23

1. lives
2. teeth
3. geese
4. leaves
5. children
6. heroes
7. people
8. oxen
9. mice
10. scarves

Minute 24

1. dog's tooth
2. Riley's pencils
3. home's roof
4. owl's wings
5. ice-cream's flavour
6. jumper's tears
7. Luci's car
8. television's remote
9. Michele's keys
10. Happy Burger's burgers

Minute 25

1. girls' parents
2. soldiers' uniforms
3. children's books
4. boys' bikes
5. My grandparents' farm
6. dogs' toys
7. models' faces
8. geese's eggs
9. men's rafts
10. wolves' prey

Minute 26

1. We
2. They
3. He
4. She
5. We
6. They
7. It
8. we
9. He
10. they

Minute 27

1. them
2. me
3. us
4. her
5. him
6. it
7. them
8. it
9. him
10. it

Minute 28

1. proper nouns: Mr Duncan, High Museum
2. common noun: bus
proper noun: Monday
3. common nouns: teacher, paintings
proper nouns: Monet
4. common nouns: mother, painting, lounge
proper noun: Monet
5. common noun: artefacts
proper noun: Laci
6. common nouns: cameras, museum
7. proper noun: Mrs Jones
8. common nouns: museum, lunch
proper noun: Hyde Park
9. common noun: blankets
proper nouns: Ahn, Staci
10. common nouns: boys, football

Minute 29

1. bear
2. bears
3. glasses
4. box
5. sister
6. mother
7. dolls
8. Barbie®
9. earrings
10. case

Minute 30

1. loaves
2. wolves
3. children
4. lives
5. teeth
6. women
7. cacti/cactuses
8. sheep
9. knives
10. people

Minute 31

1. the candle's light
2. the children's uniforms
3. the kangaroo's pouch
4. my mother's necklace
5. the calves' food
6. the netballers' bibs
7. the parents' car
8. the girl's picture
9. the pupils' teacher
10. the bandleader's trumpet

Minute 32

1. She
2. it
3. We
4. him
5. He

6. They
7. He
8. them
9. her
10. He

Minute 33

Answers may be in any order.

1–10. smell, destroy, migrate, build, dive, breathe, drag, slam, collapse, trample

Minute 34

1. snores
2. sneezed, received
3. purred, came
4. bounces
5. strode
6. cheered, came
7. put
8. see, smile
9. barks
10. are perched

Minute 35

1. lives
2. owned
3. competes
4. travelling
5. sleep
6. helps
7. watch
8. reassures
9. waiting
10. won

Minute 36

1. kicked
2. changed
3. bowed
4. disappeared
5. greeted
6. hurried
7. knelt or kneeled
8. measured
9. observed
10. promised

Minute 37

1. yes
2. no
3. yes
4. yes
5. yes
6. no
7. yes
8. no
9. yes
10. no

Minute 38

1. drove, driven
2. flew, flown
3. began, begun
4. rode, ridden
5. rang, rung
6. threw, thrown
7. wrote, written

Prim-Ed Publishing®

Minute answer key

8. told, told
9. took, taken
10. shook, shaken

Minute 39
1. admit
2. applauded
3. carrying
4. cheering
5. cried
6. disagree
7. invite
8. frightened
9. encouraged
10. guess

Minute 40
1. be
2. am
3. is
4. was
5. are
6. were
7. seemed or was
8. feel
9. am
10. are

Minute 41
1. is or was
2. was
3. were
4. am
5. had or has
6. will
7. were
8. have or had
9. are or were
10. has or had

Minute 42
Answers will vary.

Minute 43
1. receiving, received
2. destroying, destroyed
3. planning, planned
4. marrying, married
5. sniffing, sniffed
6. singing, sang
7. swimming, swam
8. carrying, carried
9. climbing, climbed
10. tasting, tasted

Minute 44
1. awakened
2. drew
3. ran
4. swept
5. teach
6. understood
7. wept
8. said
9. saw
10. forgotten

Minute 45
1. yes
2. yes
3. yes

4. no, scared
5. no, grow
6. yes
7. no, are
8. yes
9. yes
10. no, running

Minute 46
1. helping
2. linking
3. linking
4. helping
5. helping
6. helping
7. helping
8. linking
9. helping
10. helping

Minute 47
1. adjectives: bright, excellent
   nouns: girl, job
2. adjectives: four, small
   noun: apples
3. adjective: Unhappy
   noun: Fran
4. adjective: dreadful
   noun: day
5. adjectives: clumsy, huge nouns: puppy, feet
6. adjective: tall
   noun: building
7. adjective: nearby
   noun: park
8. adjective: gourmet
   noun: restaurant
9. adjective: delicious
   noun: chocolate ice-cream
10. adjective: cold
    noun: water

Minute 48
1. faster, fastest
2. greater, greatest
3. softer, softest
4. quicker, quickest
5. slower, slowest
6. taller, tallest
7. lower, lowest
8. clumsier, clumsiest
9. shorter, shortest
10. smoother, smoothest

Minute 49
1. adverb: excitedly
   verb: put
2. adverb: quickly
   verb: dart
3. adverb: gracefully
   verb: skate
4. adverb: bravely
   verb: did
5. adverb: happily
   verb: clapped
6. adverb: softly
   verb: played

7. adverb: loudly
   verb: shrieked
8. adverb: carefully
   verb: stepped
9. adverb: wisely
   verb: wore
10. adverb: cautiously
    verb: skated

Minute 50
1. forward
2. usually
3. never
4. nearby
5. After
6. somewhere
7. forever
8. away
9. late
10. now

Minute 51
1. tricycle
2. unhappy
3. megaphone
4. autograph
5. return
6. impossible
7. midnight
8. disappear
9. preview
10. nonfiction

Minute 52
Possible answers.
1. childish
2. comfortable or comforter
3. wonderful
4. friendship
5. actor or action
6. government or governor
7. kindness, kinder or kindest
8. protection, protectable or protector
9. teacher or teachable
10. smartest, smarter or smartness

Minute 53
1. yes
2. no
3. no
4. no
5. no
6. no
7. yes
8. yes
9. no
10. no

Minute 54
Only relevant section of sentence is shown.
1. Judy, please
2. Even though it had been awhile,
3. No, I
4. Because my favourite

hobby is fishing,
5. The skinny, furry
6. Yes, I
7. Dita, Karen and Lucy
8. First, Dita will take out a knife, the cream cheese, salmon and bread.
9. Next, Karen will spread the cream cheese and place the salmon on the soft bread.
10. Last, the girls will eat their sandwiches, drink milk and play board games.

Minute 55
1. Dr A Jones
2. 23 Aug.
3. WC Handy
4. Second St
5. Mr JL Shaw
6. Gen. CE Barkley
7. 12 Oct.
8. 12 Village Dr.
9. Capt. DH Holmes
10. London, UK

Minute 56
1. adjectives: beautiful, best
   nouns: mother, chicken salad
2. adjectives: smoked, hot
   nouns: chicken, fire
3. adjective: younger, tasty
   noun: sister, chicken salad sandwiches
4. adjectives: older, tiny
   nouns: brother, bites
5. adjectives: hardworking, delicious
   nouns: dad, salad
6. adjectives: caring, tasty
   nouns: mum, salad
7. happier, happiest
8. scrawnier, scrawniest
9. newer, newest
10. trickier, trickiest

Minute 57
1. adverb: closely
   verb: observed
2. adverb: carefully
   verb: removed
3. adverb: often
   verb: rains
4. adverb: high
   verb: flew
5. adverb: rarely
   verb: travel
6. adverb: finally
   verb: understood
7. adverb: well
   verb: plays

Minute answer key

8. adverb: terribly
   verb: embarrassed
9. adverb: willingly
   verb: discussed
10. adverb: Today
    verb: read

Minute 58
1. prefix
2. suffix
3. suffix
4. suffix
5. prefix
6. suffix
7. suffix
8. prefix
9. prefix
10. prefix

Minute 59
1. no
2. no
3. yes
4. yes
5. yes
6. yes
7. yes
8. no
9. no
10. yes

Minute 60
1. aka
2. Dr T Jackson
3. 15 Sept.
4. Prof. Snape
5. USA
6. BBC
7. Miss AC Peters
8. Capt. Hardaway
9. PM Tuffin
10. 17 Dec.

Minute 61
1. lighthouse
2. teamwork
3. matchmaker
4. backdrop
Answers may be in any order.
5–10. firefighter
      championship
      thunderstorm
      countdown
      drawstring
      foreground

Minute 62
1. should have
2. need not
3. who will or who shall
4. will not
5. let us
6. you are
7. does not
8. cannot
9. could have
10. he will or he shall

Minute 63
1. construct
2. haste
3. transport
4. remark
5. shy
6. thin
7. clumsy
8. ache
9. error
10. leave

Minute 64
1. ugly
2. full
3. friendly
4. begin
5. same
6. together
7. inactive
8. melt
9. disappear
10. talkative

Minute 65
1. meet, meat
2. principal, principle
3. buy, by
4. Sunday, sundae
5. knew, new
6. rein, rain
7. blew, blue
8. maid, made
9. so, sew
10. weather, whether

Minute 66
1. no, to
2. yes
3. yes
4. yes
5. no, two
6. yes
7. yes
8. no, too
9. yes
10. yes

Minute 67
1. There
2. their
3. there
4. There
5. they're
6. there
7. their
8. there
9. They're
10. Their

Minute 68
1. no, your
2. yes
3. no, your
4. yes
5. no, you're
6. yes
7. yes
8. no, you're
9. no, your

10. yes

Minute 69
1. well
2. well
3. good
4. good
5. good
6. good
7. well
8. well
9. good
10. well

Minute 70
1. affect
2. effect
3. effect
4. affect
5. affect
6. effect
7. affect
8. affect
9. effect
10. affect

Minute 71
1. accept
2. except
3. except
4. accept
5. except
6. except
7. accept
8. except
9. accept
10. accept

Minute 72
1. grasshopper
2. playmate
3. snowman
4. blackbird
5. firefighter
6. aircraft
7. toothbrush
8. wheelchair
9. nightgown
10. raincoat

Minute 73
1. I'd
2. aren't
3. they'll
4. you've
5. wouldn't
6. mustn't
7. they're
8. doesn't
9. I'm
10. isn't

Minute 74
1. S
2. A
3. H
4. A
5. S
6. A
7. A

8. H
9. S
10. H

Minute 75
1. no, their
2. yes
3. no, their
4. no, too
5. yes
6. yes
7. no, your
8. yes
9. no, to
10. no, They're

Minute 76
1. good
2. well
3. well
4. good
5. good
6. well
7. good
8. well
9. good
10. well

Minute 77
1. affected
2. effect
3. accept
4. except
5. effect
6. accepted
7. except
8. affect
9. accept
10. effect

Minute 78
1. lose
2. loose
3. loose
4. lose
5. lose
6. loose
7. yes
8. no
9. yes
10. yes

Minute 79
1. chose
2. choose
3. choose
4. chose
5. choose
6. chose
7. choose
8. chose
9. chose or choose
10. choose

Minute 80
1. its
2. It's
3. it's
4. it's
5. it's
6. its

Prim-Ed Publishing®

Minute answer key

7. It's
8. its
9. its
10. it's

Minute 81
1. yes
2. yes
3. no
4. yes
5. yes
6. yes
7. no
8. no
9. no
10. yes

Minute 82
1. neither
2. nowhere
3. not
4. Nobody
5. No
6. none
7. nothing
8. never or not
9. None
10. nowhere, not, or never

Minute 83
1. no; the
2. yes
3. yes
4. no; an
5. no; the
6. the
7. an
8. a
9. a
10. the

Minute 84
1. about
2. of
3. after
4. behind
5. instead of
6. into
7. Together with
8. Between
9. By
10. in

Minute 85
1. lose
2. loose
3. choose
4. chose
5. choose
6. lose
7. loose
8. chose
9. lose
10. chose

Minute 86
1. then
2. then
3. than
4. than
5. than

6. It's
7. its
8. it's
9. it's
10. its

Minute 87
1. no
2. yes
3. yes
4. no
5. no
Answers may vary. Possible answers listed.
6. barely
7. not
8. scarcely
9. no-one
10. hardly

Minute 88
1. a
2. an
3. a
4. a
5. an
6. an
7. a
8. an
9. an
10. a

Minute 89
1. Without
2. on
3. out
4. at
5. Because of
6. next
7. above
8. by
9. next to
10. over

Minute 90
1. P
2. V
3. N
4. A
5. A
6. N
7. P
8. A
9. V
10. N

Minute 91
1. no
2. yes
3. no
4. no
5. yes
6. yes
7. no
8. yes
9. no
10. yes

Minute 92
1. their, there
2. miss, missed
3. doesn't, don't
4. to, two
5. accept, except
6. blew, blue
7. You're, Your
8. seen, saw
9. maid, made
10. won't, want

Minute 93
1. CS
2. CS
3. CP
4. CS
5. CP
6. CP
7. CS
8. CS
9. CP
10. CP

Minute 94
1. good, well
2. its, it's
3. Their, There
4. She, Her
5. A, An
6. Him, His
7. Gina bought the doughnuts from Mr Smith's doughnut shop.
8. We moved to London, England from Madrid, Spain.
9. May we go to Mount Buffalo National Park on Saturday?
10. Mrs Brock was my favourite teacher at Gawler Primary School.

Minute 95
1. F
2. S
3. F
4. F
5. bawl, ball
6. board, bored
7. in, Inn
8. knight, night
9. write, right
10. wait, weight

Minute 96
1. They
2. We
3. She
4. He
5. their
6. it
7. imperative
8. interrogative
9. declarative
10. exclamatory

Minute 97
1. desert
2. streams
3. river
4. rain
5. animals
6. linking
7. linking
8. helping
9. linking
10. helping

Minute 98
1. pouted
2. snatch
3. glared
4. march
5. shrieking
6. clung
7. dodge
8. winced
9. chuckle
10. hummed

Minute 99
1–6. *May be in any order.*
ballroom,
lipstick,
however,
nobody,
bookshelf,
spotlight
7. yes
8. yes
9. yes
10. yes

Minute 100
1. no, took
2. yes
3. yes
4. no, discussed
5. no, made
6. If Maggie calls, tell her to come an hour earlier.
7. Jackson can play the drums, the tambourine, the flute, and the guitar.
8. Can we eat dinner, go to the cinema, go bowling, and perhaps play pool?
9. Hira, please don't forget to put the potato salad in the fridge.
10. Watch out for the dog crossing the road!